why poetry matters

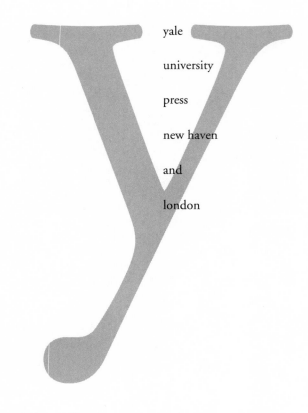

yale

university

press

new haven

and

london

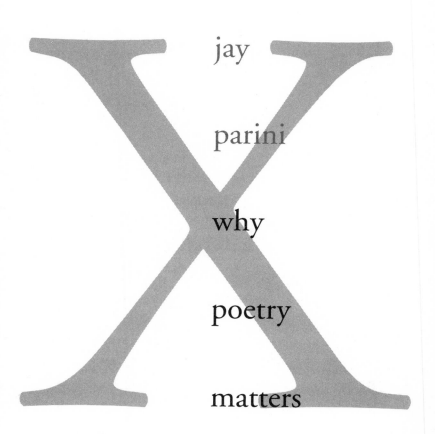

jay

parini

why

poetry

matters

A Caravan book. For more information, visit www.caravanbooks.org.

Designed by Nancy Ovedovitz and set in Adobe Garamond type by Integrated Publishing Solutions. Printed in the United States of America.

Library of Congress Cataloging-in-Publication Data
Parini, Jay.
Why poetry matters / Jay Parini.
    p.   cm. — (Why X matters)
Includes bibliographical references and index.
ISBN 978-0-300-12423-1 (alk. paper)
1. Poetry.   I. Title.
PN1031.P34 2008
808.1—dc22   2007036452

A catalogue record for this book is available from the British Library.

The paper in this book meets the guidelines for permanence and durability of the Committee on Production Guidelines for Book Longevity of the Council on Library Resources.

10 9 8 7 6 5 4 3 2 1

also by jay parini

Singing in Time (poems)
Theodore Roethke: An American Romantic (criticism)
The Love Run (novel)
Anthracite Country (poems)
The Patch Boys (novel)
An Invitation to Poetry (textbook)
Town Life (poems)
The Last Station (novel)
Bay of Arrows (novel)
John Steinbeck (biography)
Benjamin's Crossing (novel)
Some Necessary Angels: Essays on Writing and Politics
House of Days (poetry)
Robert Frost (biography)
The Apprentice Lover (novel)
One Matchless Time: A Life of William Faulkner
The Art of Teaching
The Art of Subtraction: New and Selected Poems

For Devon, who matters even more

contents

preface

Life is energy, and energy is creativity. And even when individuals
pass on, the energy is retained in the work of art, locked in it and
awaiting release if only someone will take the time and the care to
unlock it.

MARIANNE MOORE

Poetry doesn't matter to most people. That is, most people don't
write it, don't read it, and don't have any idea why anybody
would spend valuable time doing such a thing. The culture is
clamorous, with a television blaring in most living rooms, maga-
zines proliferating, and earphones downloading a great deal of
garbage into the heads of millions on the subways and byways of
the world. There is little time for concentration, or a space
wherein the still, small voice of poetry can be heard. It could be
argued, of course, that most people get their poetry in the lyrics
of songs. I would, myself, see Bob Dylan as a genuine poet, al-
though even there the tune carries as much meaning as the words,
or (at least) helps to position the words. Poetry—the kind you

read slowly to yourself, on the page—demands more of the listener, the reader. And it matters for many reasons, some of which I discuss in these pages.

From the outset, philosophers have regarded language as the key to philosophic understanding, and philosophers and linguists have written widely on language and its role in shaping thought. My touchstone for an understanding of poetic language—that highly distinct form of kinetic language, which appeals to the ear and the eye of the reader—is Ralph Waldo Emerson, whose essays I have reread throughout my life, with deep and persistent gratitude. Emerson is, for me, the fountainhead of American poetry, and his ideas have shaped the way poets from Walt Whitman and Emily Dickinson through Adrienne Rich, Charles Wright, Mary Oliver, and Louise Glück have thought about the nature of their art, especially in terms of language as a kind of echo-chamber in which the origins of words (often lost over time) enhance their current denotations and connotations. Often unconsciously, the root meanings of words add resonance and meaning to the language of the poem.

Emerson was a mystic of sorts, and his philosophy of language is founded on the traditional dualism of matter and spirit, a distinction that more recent philosophers, from Ludwig Wittgenstein to Richard Rorty, have worked to deconstruct. Nevertheless, every human being knows the difference between words and things: a fundamental rift that cannot easily be overcome. This gulf gestures to larger differences between mental images and "real" images, between spirit and nature. Poets have always been obsessed by these gaps and differences, and have explored them in a thousand ways.

The complex issue of voice also obsesses poets. Young poets try to cultivate their own voice. But what exactly is this magical thing, its gold panned for in the stream of common language? How does a poet's voice differ from the larger voice, or voices, of the culture, which are loud and insistent, often overwhelming? Can you drown out MTV? Or CNN? Or Fox? How does a poet's voice relate to the development of his or her persona or mask: the self that is created through language? I will argue in these pages that poetry matters, in part, because of voice.

It also matters because of metaphor, one of the essential forms of thought. Robert Frost suggested (with his usual sly wit) that a person uneducated in the operations of metaphor was not safe in the world, should not even be let out of doors. Poetry, for me, is important because it refines our ability to make comparisons, to understand how far one can ride a metaphor before it breaks down. There are all sorts of implications for this, some of them harshly political, as when politicians actually plunge us into illegal wars because of dangerously inept metaphors, which reflect foolish or ill-considered thinking. I quite agree with Frost that poetry offers a solid form of education, giving its readers access to metaphorical thought, its operations and dynamics.

Poetry is, of course, a traditional art form, and poets ignore the traditions of poetry at their peril. Without a fairly thorough grounding in the conventions of verse—rhythms and meters, forms, figures of speech, and so forth—it is almost impossible for a poet to achieve anything original. This is one of the paradoxes considered in this book: how the "individual talent," as T. S. Eliot described it, operates in relation to "the tradition." I suggest that originality depends on a deep understanding of tradition, this living organism that Eliot himself describes as something transmogrified before our eyes each day, as new work is added, thus reshaping the boundaries of poetic expression.

The natural boundaries of verse preoccupy most poets, who gradually come to understand the useful and affirming limits of their art. Although most poetry written after the mid-twentieth century is "free verse," as anyone will know, I would argue that formless poetry does not really exist, as poets inevitably create patterns in language that replicate forms of experience. Poetry in this sense becomes "useful" in that it allows consciousness itself to emerge within the grid of the poem. Reality inheres in the language, and the silent world sounds in the margins. Often enough, poetry gives voice to what is not usually said, and in this sense it becomes "political."

The politics of poetry is a delicate matter. It remains true that a lot of poetry has no overt connection to anything that we might call political, but poets who willfully ignore the world around them risk marginality. Poets have to "read" the world, to respond to it viscerally, and to summon images of that world for readers. Poetry is not sloganeering, and when poets directly confront a particular political crisis they need to do so carefully, even warily. They rarely put forward direct solutions to problems. Instead, they offer a kind of understanding that is distinct, as well as useful, by creating a language adequate to the experience of their readers. In this sense, poetry matters because it can waken us to realities that fall into the realm of the political.

It also matters because of the way it evokes the natural world. Entire books have been written about poetry and nature, a tradition that stretches from the pastoral poets of classical Greece and Rome to Robert Frost and beyond. Poets approach nature in highly individual ways, and few of them exhibit the same attitudes. But there is considerable agreement among them that poetic language is intimately connected to natural objects. Poets have always returned to nature for inspiration, as when Louise Glück in "Flowering Plum" writes: "In spring from the black branches of the flowering plum tree / the woodthrush issues its routine / message of survival." These messages of survival abound in nature, and poets remain alert to them. Poetry therefore returns us, through language, to the natural world, which of late has been so threatened by environmental degradation from global warming, industrial pollution, and other offenses. Here, again, the political aspects of poetry rise to the fore, as poetry reminds us that we must treasure the earth and all its glories, and work to see that none of these things are destroyed.

Spirit operates in nature, as Emerson suggested, and poetry could be viewed as a form of religious thought. Eliot's *Four Quartets,* a favorite sequence of mine, offers a firmly religious, ecumenical vision, drawing on Christian, Hindu, Buddhist, and many other religious and philosophical traditions, and it raises some broad questions: What is the nature of this world in which we find ourselves? Does it have a "meaning" or purpose? What does poetry teach us about the apprehension of time, about our place in the universe? How do poets use the tradition of inspirational writing—the scriptures—to help them to live their lives? In my view, Eliot boldly addresses these questions in poetry that represents a kind of high-water mark in twentieth-century poetry. I have relied on these poems to understand my own life and to think about poetry not as a literary critic but as a human being who looks to poems for guidance. The language of poetry can, I believe, save us. It can ground us in spiritual and moral realities, offering the consolations of philosophy, teaching us how to speak about our lives, and how—indeed—to live them.

For nearly forty years, I have begun each day with a book of poems before me as I sit over breakfast with a mug of tea. I don't think I could get through my days without these poems, which I read again and again. Poetry cannot be read, I would argue; it can only be reread. For me, it is a continuation of the holy scriptures, the kind of language one studies for insights and inspiration, for spiritual direction, for correction. Poets write in the line of prophecy, and their work teaches us how to live. The language of poetry, when properly absorbed, becomes part of our private vocabulary, our way of moving through the world. Poetry matters, and without it we can live only partially, not fully conscious of the possibilities (emotional and intellectual) that life affords.

Aiming for that Common Reader whom Virginia Woolf once imagined as the ideal audience for her essays, I have tried, when possible, to avoid anything that smacks of specialist jargon, believing that the sort of technical language that critics often use these days is both unnecessary and elitist, a way of drawing the wagons around the fire, as if attack were almost certain. Such paranoia is pointless. I always tell my students that one of the blessings of poetry is that it has no commercial value, no position in the marketplace. But it nevertheless possesses great value for those who understand its possibilities, its range and reasons. I try to break what Wallace Stevens once called the "bread of faithful speech" in these pages, and to repeat in a softly insistent voice to anyone who cares to listen: take, eat.

1 defending poetry

Poets are the unacknowledged legislators of the world.

PERCY BYSSHE SHELLEY

Poets are the legislators of the unacknowledged world.

GEORGE OPPEN

Poets have been on the run since Plato announced in the *Republic* (fourth century B.C.) that "there is an ancient quarrel between philosophy and poetry." Speaking in the voice of Socrates, he argued that poets should be kicked out of the ideal republic. They were no good because they imitated nature, which is itself an imitation of the ideal world—a heavenly kingdom of "reality" that surpasses these imperfect reflections everywhere presented to the human senses. With metaphysical slyness, Plato maintained that the poet "is an imitator, and therefore, like all other imitators, he is thrice removed from the king and from the truth."[1] (The "king" here is the ideal form.) But there were other, perhaps more practical, reasons for getting the poets out of the way.

The business of the state, in Plato's view, was to protect the young from corruption, and poets corrupt them by exciting feelings that do not promote decent and patriotic behavior. (One of the ironies here is that Socrates himself—a fearless teacher of the young—was condemned to death for corrupting the youth of Athens with his free-thinking ideas. Indeed, I often wonder what Socrates would have thought if, coming back from the dead, he had read the words that his student Plato had put into his mouth.) Even Homer, chief among the Greek poets, was not spared criticism. "Friend Homer," Socrates quips with a condescending smile, "if you are able to discern what pursuits make men better or worse in private or public life, tell us what State was ever better governed by your help?" The implied answer, of course, is "none." Homer may have entertained and titillated his audience, but he assisted nobody in governing a state. He may even have made things more difficult for them by stimulating feelings that could not easily be contained and by implicitly questioning the wisdom of the gods and earthly rulers. Certainly nobody who has read the *Iliad* (I remember actually weeping over its pages when I first read it, in college) has come away from the experience believing that war is a good, useful, and rational thing, or that its pursuit is anything but destructive and evil.

Socrates (or Plato's fictionalized version of his teacher) whips himself into a frenzy over poetry in the *Republic*, arguing that poets promote petty emotions such as "lust and anger and all the other affections, of desire and pain and pleasure, which are held to be inseparable from every action." He complains that poetry "feeds and waters the passions instead of drying them up." So poetry militates against "happiness and virtue" by softening up its readers, making them prey to all sorts of dangerous and corrupting emotions. Only "the hymns of the gods and praises of famous men" are considered useful for the state and therefore satisfactory as themes for poets. "If you go beyond this," Socrates warns, "and allow the honeyed muse to enter, either in epic or lyric verse, not law and the reason of mankind, which by common consent have ever been deemed best, but pleasure and pain will be the rulers in our State."

Plato did not manage to sink the art of poetry, but the light of suspicion has continued to shine on poets ever since he raised these objections. Poets are the wayward ones, the voices of protest against authority, the defenders of powerful feeling over fierce intellection, the abettors of all forms of disgusting and irreverent behavior. They lead the young astray, offering them a swig of wine, luring them into opium dens. They promote sensuality, even free love. They denounce presidents and prime ministers and generally ridicule governments as well as the educational establishment. Their language is as loose as their morals. When the popular audience today in the United States thinks of a poet, Allen Ginsberg comes to mind: the bearded hippie, antiwar activist, and sexual "deviant" who wrote, in "America": "Go fuck yourself with your atom bomb." To a degree, all this mistrust can be traced to Plato and his dismissive views of poetry.

Plato set the terms of the argument, initiating a dialogue that continues to this day. Among his first interlocutors were Aristotle, Horace, and Longinus—the most prominent of ancient defenders of poetry. Aristotle uses the term broadly to include drama as well as verse. Like Plato, he regards poets as imitators of nature, but this does not strike him as a problem. The music of poetry attracted him, as it has always attracted its admirers. He suggests that "rhythm, tune, and meter" are essential to poetry, its foundation, and locates the urge to write poems in two places that lie "deep in our nature." There is first the instinct for imitation: we naturally wish to reproduce things observed or felt. This is what separates us from other living creatures. Second, we have an instinctive love of harmony and rhythm, which is why we perk up when we hear a drumbeat in the distance, why our foot begins to tap when a catchy tune is struck. He writes: "Persons, therefore, starting with this natural gift developed by degrees their special attitudes, till their rude improvisations gave birth to poetry."[2]

In other words, as human beings we want to replicate things that we sense, and we like to do so in pleasing ways. Poets are simply people who seek to perfect this form of imitation. Aristotle steps neatly around the question of content in poetry, unlike Horace, the Roman poet and friend of the great emperor Augustus. Horace had Plato firmly in mind when he wrote his famous defense of poetry, the *Ars poetica,* in the second decade B.C. "To have good sense," he writes confidently, "is the first principle and fountain of writing well." Good sense requires a sense of moderation, a feel for what might encourage youthful readers to behave in decent ways. "The Socratic papers will direct you in the choice of your subjects," he tells young writers, referring to Plato's Socrates. The reader of poems must, above all, learn "what he owes his country, and what to his friends." He must also understand "with what affection a parent, a brother, and a stranger, are to be loved," and know as well "what is the duty of a senator, what of a judge; what the duties of a general sent out to war." Horace implies that poetry is useful because it can both teach and delight at the same time and therefore has utilitarian value.[3]

Like Plato and Aristotle, Horace sees the poet as an "imitator of nature," but he is unwilling to dismiss the entire art of poetry on these grounds: "I should direct the learned imitator to have regard for the mode of nature and manners, and thence draw his expressions to life." In other words, the poet's imitation of nature (human nature as well as the natural world) must approximate the "mode" of what he or she imitates. That is, poetry must not distort reality. It must conjure an accurate representation of everyday life, what can be seen and heard and felt, and readers must judge the accuracy of these representations.

Horace ends his essay with a warning to readers: "Those who are wise avoid a mad poet, and are afraid to touch him." (In other words, don't listen to the likes of Allen Ginsberg.) That such words should come from one of the major Roman poets is worth noting. This attitude defines Horace and his poetic project. As Gordon Williams observes, Horace was already an influential poet at the time this essay appeared, and he was writing—like most poets—to justify his own art. *Ars poetica* is "a work characterized by the imprint of an individual personality which dominates the tone and controls the material." Its relevance, says Williams, "adds up to an attitude to poetry, an expression of professionalism and a sense of critical standards, a hatred of humbug and of too easily won approval."[4]

That Horace addressed a select audience of sophisticated, court-centered readers is obvious in everything he did. He is, after all, the man who wrote (not without irony), "I despise the vulgar masses, and push them away."[5] There is everywhere in his work a sense that poetry should educate the young in the manners and sentiments appropriate for those who might become statesmen. Such an attitude is not uncommon throughout classical Greece and Rome, where the drumbeats of Plato could always be heard in the distance. Needless to say, poets have rarely conformed to thematic constraints in ways that would have satisfied Plato. From Homer onward, they have written movingly about the ruins of war, about the demands of conscience, about bodily love and the seductions of nature. They have occasionally gone way over the edge in describing religious emotions, reaching for mystical heights, contesting the gods as well as praising them. In general, passions are rarely kept on a leash.

Toward the end of the first century A.D., the critic known as Longinus (of whom almost nothing is known) wrote "On the Sublime," an influential treatise on what makes for intense feeling in poetry and prose. By "the sublime," he refers to all that is noble and grand, generous and affecting. What is sublime is also that which continues to inspire over time, across cultures and languages. Longinus writes: "For that is really great which bears a repeated examination, and which is difficult or rather impossible to withstand, and the memory of which is strong and hard to efface."[6] The point has never been put more boldly, to greater effect.

The influence of Longinus is hard to overestimate. He put a finger on the use of poetry and defended it against all detractors, especially Plato. His sentiments played out in various ways in the centuries that followed, but there is no doubt about his belief in the powers of language to transform reality, to affect readers in deep and permanent ways. For him poetry makes it possible for people to live more intensely, with a greater awareness of the life that confronts them. It helps them to cope with the vagaries of their existence. Poetry lifts them onto higher ground, where they can survey the ruins of civilization with a perspective that allows for equanimity, even elation.

The wisdom of the ancients was lost during the medieval period, the "dark ages." That is the traditional view, and it bears some resemblance to the truth, given that the writings of the Greek classical authors were not widely available until the twelfth century. A revival of learning occurred during the early modern period, when a rebirth ("renaissance") of interest in classical literature occurred. One of the big ideas about poetry that was revived was the notion that it could both "teach and delight" its readers, as Horace put it. A number of poets responded to this renewal of interest, including Dante, who wrote the *Divine Comedy* in the early fourteenth century. He ranks with Homer and Shakespeare among the poets who appeal to readers across the barriers of time and language. Indeed, T. S. Eliot called him "the most *universal* of poets in the modern languages."[7]

Eliot's defense of Dante has a quality of special pleading to it, but one must note the obvious: poetry had a marvelous practitioner in Dante, and it is always in specific examples that an age comes to believe in the power of poetry to transform lives, to make readers see themselves and their world more clearly, and to lead those readers toward a more vivid and conscious life. Poetry extends the boundaries of thought by extending the boundaries of expression itself. Poets articulate thoughts and feelings in ways that clarify both; they hold a mirror of sorts up to the mind if not to the world, and their poems reflect our deepest imaginings, our hopes for ourselves and our society. Poetry offers concrete images that draw into their figures a reflection and embodiment of our lives. At its best, poetry is a language adequate to our experience.

During the Renaissance, a wide range of philosophers and critics came to the defense of poetry. Perhaps the most famous articulation of the case occurred in the "Apology for Poetry" by Sir Philip Sidney. An English gentleman par excellence, Sidney did everything right: born rich, he rode a horse, managed a large estate, married well, and commanded men in battle (he died soon after the Battle of Arnheim in 1586, as a consequence of having taken a musket ball in the leg). He was himself a splendid poet and a scholar as well, having studied the classics at Oxford. Like a masterful attorney, he could marshal evidence on a grand scale, and his treatise reads like a legal defense, an elegant one, with arguments based on his reading of (now obscure) writers such as Erasmus, Thomas More, Julius Scaliger, Peter Ramus, and Pietro Bembo. The range of his learning was not only exhaustive, it was exhausting, and one can easily recoil from Sidney's methodical approach, tantamount to overkill. Nevertheless, he defends poetry in ways that have profoundly influenced modern thinking about the art and its use in the world.

Drafted in 1580, the "Apology" was published in its current form after Sidney's death. It argues that "of all writers under the sun, the poet is the least liar."[8] Once again, Plato is the opponent, the man who considered poets liars because they imitated nature, which is itself an imitation of the ideal. As Sidney explains, poetry creates "fictional" statements that are "true." They are not meant as literal copies of higher or ideal reality. Any statement is provisional, as Ramus argued before him. For Sidney, poetry has much to do with self-fashioning, with creating an identity. It offers a unique picture of the world, one that is not wholly dependent on verifiable reality; it achieves its own reality, which cannot easily be dismissed. In this, Sidney reflects rather sophisticated "modern" ideas about language and its relation to reality that would have been familiar to educated readers in the late sixteenth century.

Sidney is not terribly worried about the Platonic problem of imitation (mimesis). "There is no art delivered unto mankind that hath not the works of nature for his principal object, without which they could not consist, and on which they so depend, as they become actors and players, as it were, of what nature will have set forth." God imagines the world, and human beings—who were created in the image of God—replicate this process. The poet becomes godlike, creating realities or "fictions" much as God has done. But whereas scientists as well as historians must somehow attempt to approximate reality in their prose, poets create their own truths, which are not literal and therefore cannot be subject to the criticisms that Plato and others would force upon them. The poet, says Sidney, works through metaphors. Scientists, historians, and philosophers do this as well, whether or not they acknowledge it. Here Sidney gives poets the upper hand because they know what they are doing. They work in metaphors self-consciously, having learned how. Indeed, Sidney lifts the poet well above these others, who are tied to literal realities that they can only imitate badly and probably distort. The poet furnishes the world with fresh knowledge, combining the gift of speech (*oratio*) with the gift of reason (*ratio*), creating figures on the page that become a substance themselves, interpreting reality as much as reflecting it. The poet is "full of virtue-breeding delightfulness, and void of no gift that ought to be in the noble name of learning." The whole question of imitation melts away here, irrelevant. In this, Sidney foreshadows a key aspect of postmodern thought, with its emphasis on truth as a subjective creation, unverifiable but needing no verification.

Modern ideas about the value of poetry have their deepest roots in the Romantic era, that wonderfully productive period in the arts that began in Germany in the eighteenth century and spread to England and America in the nineteenth. It was a movement that prized self-expression and preferred passionate feelings to dry, intellectual arguments. Romantic artists stood on the edge of society, offering critiques and bold counterexamples. They mistrusted authority. Most important, they celebrated the natural world, which they regarded as holy, almost a spirit in itself. They moved well beyond the classical idea that poetry should instruct the young in good morals. In his preface to *Lyrical Ballads* (1800), William Wordsworth—among the most influential of the English Romantic poets—puts forward a few essential ideas about poetry, ideas that have hardly shifted in two centuries. First, Wordsworth regards poetry as "the spontaneous overflow of powerful feeling" that takes the form of "emotion recollected in tranquility." In this, poetry stands in opposition to science and history. Talking about the origins of poetry, he speculates that the earliest poets "wrote from passion excited by real events; they wrote naturally, and as men: feeling powerfully as they did, their language was daring, and figurative." Wordsworth separates poets from others on the grounds of sensibility; the poet is "endowed with more lively sensibility, more enthusiasm and tenderness." He is "pleased with his own passions and volitions" and "rejoices more than other men in the spirit of life that is in him." Finally, Wordsworth argues that the purpose of poetry is "to produce excitement in co-existence with an overbalance of pleasure." Thus poetry serves to widen the sensibilities of readers and to broaden their sympathies.[9]

In setting poets apart from others, Wordsworth invites the disdain of society. I will agree with society here, believing it foolish to think of poets as having finer and more pronounced feelings than others. They experience the same feelings as most human beings; they simply have a knack for putting feelings into words and a gift for working within the conventions of poetic expression. In most cases, they will have spent some time studying the craft of poetry, learning how to embody their emotions and refine their ideas in the language and forms we refer to as poetry.

Wordsworth's close friend Samuel Taylor Coleridge (co-author of *Lyrical Ballads*) generally shared the conception of poetry put forward in the "Preface," but he was more philosophical by nature and rooted his ideas in theories of creativity acquired by reading German philosophy and criticism of the eighteenth century (where the origins of Romantic theory will be found in such writers as Friedrich and A. W. von Schlegel, J. C. F. von Schiller, and J. G. Herder, among others.) In *Biographia Literaria* (1817), a book of literary musings that has been hugely influential, Coleridge puts forward his essential ideas about poetry, distancing himself from Wordsworth in subtle ways. "A poem is that species of composition," he writes, "which is opposed to works of science, by proposing for its immediate object pleasure, not truth; and from all other species (having this object in common with it) it is discriminated by proposing to itself such delight from the whole, as is compatible with a distinct gratification from each component part." He defines poetry in terms of poets themselves. "What is poetry?" he asks, noting that this "is so nearly the same question with, what is a poet?" He concludes: "The poet, described in *ideal* perfection, brings the whole soul of man into activity. . . . He diffuses a tone and spirit of unity, that blends, and (as it were) *fuses,* each into each, by that synthetic and magical power, to which we have exclusively appropriated the name of imagination." This power—the literary imagination—"reveals itself in the balance or reconciliation of opposite or discordant qualities."[10]

Coleridge divides the imagination into two parts, primary and secondary: "The primary IMAGINATION I hold to be the living Power and prime Agent of all human Perception, and as a repletion in the finite mind of the eternal act of creation in the infinite I AM. The secondary Imagination I consider as an echo of the former." The primary imagination is initial perception: how we assemble the world at a glance. Poetry comes into play with the secondary imagination, as the poet takes what is given by the senses, dissolves it, then reconstitutes this reality to form a counterreality. The process involves an elaborate dialectic, an interplay of reality and the imagination, that seems a bit more complicated than anything Wordsworth had in mind when he wrote about poetry as "the spontaneous overflow of powerful feeling." Coleridge describes an organic process, one that occurs naturally in the creative imagination, wherever that resides; it involves perception and destruction and reconstitution.

The organic metaphor was central to thinking about poetry during the late eighteenth and nineteenth centuries, and Coleridge often used it. As M. H. Abrams notes, Coleridge held that "literary invention involves the natural, unplanned, and unconscious process by which things grow."[11] Like a plant, the poet gathers material from the atmosphere around him and puts out branches and leaves. The poem itself, also like a plant, begins with a seed or "germ." It finds its natural or inherent shape, having assimilated materials from the atmosphere. The metaphor is powerful and remains influential among critics, who often shrink from a work of art that seems mechanical or in some way distorted; indeed, one commonly hears it suggested that a poem or play or novel should be "organic." The individual parts should work together to create a unified impression. It should be integrated, made whole.

Some critics found Wordsworth and Coleridge excessive in their regard for poetry, and one of these was Thomas Love Peacock, known mainly for his novels. In an essay called "The Four Ages of Poetry" (1820), he launches an amusing attack on Wordsworth's ideas, taking particular aim at the notion that poetry had its origins in the gestures of our primitive ancestors, who banged on drums and danced in circles around a fire, chanting. Nevertheless, he acknowledges the force of primitive poetry. "In the origin and perfection of poetry," he argues, "all the associations of life were composed of poetic materials. With us, it is decidedly the reverse." He suggests that poetry has become an anachronism in an era when science, philosophy, and economics reign supreme. Such remarks were bound to elicit criticism from poets and lovers of poetry, and they did, including an eloquent and influential defense of poetry by Peacock's friend Percy Bysshe Shelley, then at the height of his poetic powers.[12]

In "A Defence of Poetry" (1821), Shelley questions many of Peacock's assumptions, making his own exaggerated claims: "Poetry enlarges the circumference of the imagination by replenishing it with thoughts of ever new delight, which have the power of attracting and assimilating to their own nature all other thoughts, and which form new intervals and interstices whose void forever craves fresh food. Poetry strengthens the faculty which is the organ of the moral nature of man, in the same manner as exercise strengthens a limb." Using a popular analogy, he compares human beings to the Aeolian harp or wind chime. Winds blow over this passive instrument, drawing forth "their ever-changing melody." Shelley refines the analogy to suggest that people are different in that they actually harmonize the various winds, unifying them, creating new wholes from disparate elements. This is the important work of the poem: to unify otherwise fragmented experience. Shelley offers the most vigorous defense of poetry ever composed, seeing the art as the sum of all human activities. Poetry both creates "new materials of knowledge" and "engenders in the mind a desire to reproduce and arrange them according to a certain rhythm and order which may be called the beautiful and the good." Poetry is "something divine," locating the "center and circumference of knowledge." Somewhat grandly, he refers to poets as "the unacknowledged legislators of mankind," a remark that has drawn endless derision over the years.

In nineteenth-century America, Emerson, Walt Whitman, and Emily Dickinson picked up on Shelley's theme in their very different ways, yet each saw poetry as central to the human enterprise. "The poet is the Namer, or Language-maker, naming things sometimes after their appearance, sometimes after their essence, and giving to every one its own name and not another's thereby rejoicing the intellect, which delights in the detachment or boundary," writes Emerson in "The Poet" (1844). "The poets made all the words, and therefore language is the archives of history, and, if we must say it, a sort of tomb of the muses. For, though the origin of most of our words is forgotten, each word was at first a stroke of genius, and obtained currency, because for the moment it symbolized the world to the first speaker and to the hearer. The etymologist finds the deadest word to have been once a brilliant picture. Language is fossil poetry." And so the work of the poet is to refresh the language itself, returning words to their pictorial origins. Emerson surveys the vast American continent and wonders where he might find a poet equal to this plenitude.[13]

Whitman found this poet in . . . Walt Whitman, celebrating himself as the spokesman for North America, if not the whole world, in *Song of Myself*, but also in his magnificent preface to *Leaves of Grass* (1855). In this latter work he argues that anyone can appreciate the natural world, but the poet must do more than merely point to "the beauty and dignity which always attach to dumb real objects." All men and women see this luxuriance, he maintains. But the poet, above others, must "indicate the path between reality and their souls." It is in the articulation of spiritual lines between the human mind and the world of external reality that poets find their truest calling. Whitman concludes that "a great poem is for ages and ages in common and for all degrees and complexions and all departments and sects and for a woman as much as a man and a man as much as a woman. A great poem is no finish to a man or woman but rather a beginning."[14]

In her delicate, strange poems, Emily Dickinson often considered the poet's function in elevated terms. She left behind no elaborate defense of poetry in prose, although her mentor, Thomas Wentworth Higginson, recalled a comment that comes as close to a theory of poetry as anything we have by her: "If I read a book and it makes my whole body so cold no fire can ever warm me, I know that is poetry. If I feel physically as if the top of my head were taken off, I know that is poetry. These are the only ways I know it. Is there any other way?" In poem 448, she writes: "This was a Poet—It is That / Distills amazing sense / From ordinary Meanings."[15] And she placed great store by naming as well, by "saying" a poem, as in poem 1212:

A word is dead
When it is said,
Some say.
I say it just
Begins to live
That day.

. . . . .

One finds endless variations on the above themes among the poets of the twentieth century. The idea that poets assimilate various elements and unify them was given memorable expression by Eliot in his essay on the Metaphysical poets: "When a poet's mind is perfectly equipped for its work, it is constantly amalgamating disparate experience; the ordinary man's experience is chaotic, irregular, fragmentary. The latter falls in love, or reads Spinoza, and these two experiences have nothing to do with each other, or with the noise of the typewriter or the smell of cooking; in the mind of the poet these experiences are always forming new wholes."[16]

Eliot saw the poet's work as making connections to tradition, keeping it alive by constantly challenging and debating its contours. (See Chapter 5 for a full elaboration of this idea.) His poetry often reflects the spiritual crisis that came in the wake of the Great War, when sacred signs and symbols seemed devoid of meaning, "a heap of broken images." In *The Waste Land*, he sifts through the remains of civilization to find those bits and pieces of literature that had meaning for him: "These fragments I have shored against my ruins." In *Four Quartets*, his most exhilarating achievement (which I consider in detail in Chapter 9), he searches in Christian and Buddhist traditions to find "the still point of the turning world," meditating in urgent ways on the power of art itself to create a sense of order.

Eliot believed that the work of the poet was to "purify the dialect of the tribe," as he wrote in "Little Gidding," echoing a well-known line in French by Stéphane Mallarmé. This purification, for Eliot, is an act of attention to language, a way of making sure that it demonstrates an "easy commerce of the old and the new." Language moves toward stillness, toward a centered life in which the eternal demands of the spirit pour into the details of everyday life, our temporal world. In a similar vein, Robert Frost writes that his whole project as a poet was about the "deeper and deeper penetration of spirit into matter." Frost had his own version of the "still point" analogy, suggesting that poetry offered "a momentary stay against confusion."[17]

Poets often talk about their hopes for poetry, in prose as well as in their poems. In "The Monument," Elizabeth Bishop puts forward her view of art in a delicate fashion, suggesting that artworks, whether taking the shape of "a piece of sculpture, or poem, or monument," all have in common their ability to "shelter / what is within." And in her heartbreaking poem "One Art," she writes about trying to contain within the poem the endless losses, little and large, that afflict a human being. The poem ends with an address to the poet herself, in which she (with bitter irony) observes that "the art of losing's not too hard to master / though it may look like (*Write it!*) like disaster." There is a certain residual faith in the art in that fierce parenthetical command: *Write it!*

Of all poets, Wallace Stevens was the most compulsive theorist of his own art. He could apparently think of nothing else but the use of poetry. The word itself for him stood in for nearly everything created by the human mind in response to the chaos of the world. In his lecture "The Noble Rider and the Sound of Words," delivered at Princeton in 1942, when the Second World War threatened to obliterate the globe, he talks about the confrontation between reality and the imagination that forms the basis of all his poems. He laments the fact that reality, after the Great War, "became so violent." He refers to "the pressure of reality," by which he means "life in a state of violence, not physically violent, as yet, for us in America, but physically violent for millions of our friends and for still more millions of our enemies and spiritually violent, it may be said, for everyone alive."[18]

The pressure of reality is fierce, yet poetry supplies a counterpressure, pushing back against this external pressure, seeking an equilibrium—"a pressure great enough and prolonged enough to bring about the end of one era in the history of imagination and, if so, then great enough to bring about the beginning of another." He adds, "It is not that there is a new imagination but that there is a new reality"; indeed, "the pressure of reality is, I think, the determining factor in the artistic character of an era and, as well, the determining factor in the artistic character of an individual. The resistance to this pressure or its evasion in the case of individuals of extraordinary imagination cancels the pressure so far as those individuals are concerned." In this, the poet's role is simply "to help people live their lives."

Poetry, therefore, assists readers subjected to violent realities by opening their minds to fresh ways of thinking. Most famously, Stevens defines poetry as "a violence from within that protects us from a violence without. It is the imagination pressing back against the pressure of reality. It seems, in the last analysis, to have something to do with our self-preservation; and that, no doubt, is why the expression of it, the sound of its words, helps us to live our lives." And so we look for a language that embodies and "pushes back" against the outside world. Without that force of expression, there is no comfort or stability, no means of coping with the surrounding destruction and fragmentation.

Poetry is by its very nature political, although it does not necessarily advocate one policy over another, side with a particular party, raise a fist in defiance, or hold a banner in a parade of protest. Poets may do all of the above, but in their poems they supply something that comes before the polemics: a sense of direction, a spiritual grounding, a place to stand where the pressure of reality will not overcome the imagination, thus limiting possibilities.

Many poets in our violent "postwar" era have responded to the devastation in their own measure and style. Among the best of these has been Adrienne Rich, who has battled the patriarchal culture as well as the war-mongering culture—if these can be separated. She has found a crucial "dynamic between a political vision and the demand for a fresh vision of literature." She writes: "For a poem to coalesce, for a character or an action to take shape, there has to be an imaginative transformation of reality which is in no way passive." The poet must actively confront reality, in fresh language. "If the imagination is to transcend and transform experience it has to question, to challenge, to conceive of alternatives, perhaps to the very life you are living at that moment. You have to be free to play around with the notion that day might be night, love might be hate; nothing can be too sacred for the imagination to turn into its opposite or to call experimentally by another name. For writing is renaming."[19]

Poetry is certainly renaming of a kind, as Emerson observes in "The Poet." It is finding the words that connect past to present, thereby transforming the present reality from something intolerable to something one can live with, even love. The mind of the poet supplies a light to the minds of others, kindling their imaginations, helping them to live their lives. It is a confrontation, a counterpressure, an alternate world of reimagined language that informs the reality that is everywhere pressing and pulling, shouting and—in this day and age—exploding. Power, says Rich, is essential in the poet, in poetry itself; but this power "is not power of domination, but just access to sources." This means connecting readers to the history of language itself, to the history of human encounters with the violent realities that surround them, and to the history of human success in the struggle for spiritual survival. Most crucially, perhaps, poetry restores the culture to itself: mirroring what it finds there already but also sensing and embodying the higher purposes and buried ideals of that culture, granting access to hidden sources of power. Poets become, in George Oppen's twist on Shelley's famous line, "the legislators of the unacknowledged world," naming things previously unnamed, what is hidden or buried, what lies beneath the culture but nevertheless plays a huge role in shaping its sense of itself.[20]

Nobody, not even Plato, would toss out of the ideal republic the poet who could deliver on these promises. The wonder is that so many of them have indeed delivered.

2 language

Language is fossil poetry.

RALPH WALDO EMERSON

If our language is inadequate, our
vision remains formless, our
thinking and feeling are still
running in the old cycles, our
process may be "revolutionary"
but not transformative.

ADRIENNE RICH

L anguage matters, and poetic language matters a great deal. What distinguishes human beings from other animals in the vast circus of this world is their ability to put ideas into words. They can talk about their feelings and signal to one another in complex ways, indicating an immense variety of things, important or trivial. They can formulate abstract notions, some of them profound. They frame laws and constitutions that define nation states and communities, articulate social norms, and make designs for living. News of what happens passes among them swiftly in language created for such a purpose. They communicate intense personal feelings and attitudes, forming alliances of one kind or another. As all parents know, language plays a huge role in the replication of the race itself and in the way children are brought up.

In poetry, which employs a refined form of language governed by certain conventions or traditional assumptions, writers articulate moods, describe intense and powerful states of mind, and formulate ideas of considerable subtlety and rhetorical power. At its best, poetry inspires political and spiritual awareness among readers, opening the heart and mind to possibilities never quite imaginable without it. In a poem, language becomes a form of revelation, as Stevens suggests when he writes, "Description is revelation." A whole world becomes available to readers that was not there before.

Description in the compressed and kinetic mode of poetry demands a special kind of language, one that "gives to airy nothing / A local habitation and a name," as Shakespeare's Theseus says in *A Midsummer Night's Dream* (V, i). This language moves beyond the abstract language of newspapers and textbooks, being more image-centered, more precise, more suggestive. As a language adequate to our experience, poetry allows us to articulate matters of concern in such a way that they become physical, tangible, and immediate. Indeed, the finest poems become indestructible objects in their own right, taking on a life beyond the immediate circumstances of the poets who create them.

Any discussion of poetic language should be grounded in the ongoing discussion of language in general, with its roots in ancient philosophy. The study of language is a broad field, with traditional modes ranging from the study of rhetoric (language as the art of persuasion) to various philological and linguistic approaches, which often focus on syntax and grammar or the evolution of particular words. In the study of literary language, style comes into play, and critics inevitably concern themselves with value, asking, Is this writing any good? Why? More recently, critics have added a further question: In making literary judgments, can one escape subjective (ethnocentric, personal) presuppositions about what is good, not-so-good, or (God forbid!) rotten?

Modern philosophers have focused on language as a key to philosophic understanding. Ludwig Wittgenstein and Martin Heidegger, perhaps the most influential modern philosophers, consider language as the necessary medium for thought, believing that if something cannot be formulated in language, it remains beyond thought, or possibly beyond consciousness, unmediated and unrealized. But they regard language as possibility as well, as a means for gaining access to wider consciousness. As the philosopher Ilham Dilman says, "Both Wittgenstein and Heidegger have, in their different ways, shown us how much we owe the world in which we live—*le monde vécu*—the world of our engagement, to the language we speak. Heidegger speaks of language opening up a world for us—a field, a realm in which we live our lives, find the objects with which we engage, and in those engagements ourselves."[1]

In his earlier writing Wittgenstein tends to see language as a mirror of reality, with words pointing to specific objects. This notion had obvious difficulties, as signs (words, phrases, linguistic images) rarely connect so easily to a referent. Later, in *Philosophical Investigations* (1953), he rejects this idea, looking at the way language derives meaning in a social context and regarding the realities of language as somehow independent of the world itself. The assumption that language reflects reality struck him as simplistic and distorting, even in his own (rather complex) formulation of this notion; he had begun to think about the ways in which language transforms reality, embodies it, even creates it. In a sense, Wittgenstein is moving in the direction of poetics here, seeing language as substance, a means of generating realities and extending, if not shaping, consciousness.

The various approaches to language taken by philosophers after Wittgenstein are fascinating if sometimes confusing. J. L. Austin, Gilbert Ryle, and P. F. Strawson, among others, developed a mode of analytical philosophy in the middle decades of the twentieth century that has—at least in the form often referred to as ordinary language philosophy—gone out of style.[2] These philosophers, and their followers at British and American universities, looked at individual sentences closely, examining their performative aspect (how they act in the process of speech and communication), thinking about presuppositions that underlay certain utterances, engaging philosophical and logical issues of a fairly general scope. More recently, Richard Rorty has modified this analytical approach in fruitful ways by reconnecting with the tradition of American Pragmatism, which has its roots in the work of William James and C. S. Peirce. In *Philosophy and the Mirror of Nature* (1979) and *Consequences of Pragmatism* (1982), for instance, he argues that language does not hold a mirror up to nature; indeed, he finds that old metaphor debilitating and distracting. Instead, for Rorty, language offers tools for picking at reality, for dislodging shards of meaning, thus allowing us to communicate with one another in practical ways. It provides a means for coping with the world as we find it. Truth is not something one simply "discovers," whose reality is beyond challenge. Instead, one creates reality through language, and these realities cannot escape their subjective origins. Ethnocentrism, for example, will always interfere with attempts at creating reality. In this, Rorty shifts his linguistic approach away from philosophy as such, moving in overtly political directions, much to the annoyance of many critics.

Theoretical linguists, as opposed to philosophers, have usually resisted making philosophical arguments, focusing instead on the scientific description of language. Morton Bloomfield, in *Language* (1933), examines the dynamics of sentences, attempting to find an adequate means for describing languages in operation. (Two components of language that linguists such as Bloomfield examine are its phonemic and morphemic aspects: the sounds of speech in themselves and how these sounds are arranged on a string called syntax.) A revolutionary twist in the study of language occurred when Noam Chomsky, in *Syntactic Structures* (1957), began to ask questions about how language reflects innate mental structures and cognitive possibilities—that is, he began to look for direct connections between language and mind. A student of the linguist Zellig Harris, who had done pioneering work in the area of syntax (how words hang together), Chomsky wondered how a child with limited knowledge of grammar or syntax could nevertheless generate an infinite number of sentences. And he understood this question in a larger philosophical context, searching for a "universal grammar," those rules and conventions that are unspecific to a particular language but exist, as it were, in a common domain.[3]

In an essay on cognitive capacity, for example, Chomsky refers to a central question that has preoccupied philosophers of mind: "From Plato to the present time, serious philosophers have been baffled and intrigued by the question that Bertrand Russell, in one of his later works, formulated in this way: 'How comes it that human beings, whose contacts with the world are brief and personal and limited, are nevertheless able to know as much as they do know?' "[4] In a sense, the vast and complicated project of modern linguistics after Chomsky might be seen as an attempt to answer this question, although it has proved remarkably intractable.

Chomsky did innovative work in the field of what is called transformational grammar, looking at how sentences are produced. He examines the so-called deep structures of language in relation to surface structures. He opened a seminal essay called "Deep Structure, Surface Structure, and Semantic Interpretation" with his signature qualities of clarity and force: "A grammar of a language, in the sense in which I will use this term, can be loosely described as a system of rules that expresses the correspondence between sound and meaning in this language. Let us assume two given universal language independent systems of representation, a phonetic system for the specification of sound and a semantic system for the specification of meaning. As to the former, there are many concrete proposals. In the domain of semantics there are, needless to say, problems of fact and principle that have barely been approached, and there is no reasonably concrete or well-defined 'theory of semantic representation' to which one can refer."[5]

This writing may have a peculiar density for those unfamiliar with terms like *syntax*, *phonetics*, or *semantics*. Syntax, again, refers to the order of words in a sentence, and its formal study includes looking at how sentences are built, and how the bits and pieces connect. Phonetics is just the study of the noises that words produce, their physical properties, while semantics considers how these noises produce meaning in the mind of the person who hears them. With his mathematical bent, Chomsky diagrammed ways that words become sentences and looked at how sentences form consistent patterns that can be classified and examined. He guessed that deeper meanings could be found here, in that the patterns of language reflected patterns of mind. And one could even discern different levels of "depth"—a metaphor of space—in the study of language as it relates to mind. All of this, the general field called theoretical linguistics, remains a controversial way of thinking about language, but it is undeniably stimulating. And no serious student of language can avoid a confrontation with its most basic assumptions and speculations.

In a recent interview, Chomsky talked about theoretical linguistics in a larger context: "It had been recognized for centuries, by Galileo, for example, that the crucial aspect of language is discrete infinity—the capacity to create arbitrary structures of arbitrary complexity by putting together discrete items, which is rather unusual in the biological world. By the 1950s, advances in the theory of computation of algorithms and formal systems had progressed to the point where it was possible to try to articulate precisely and explicitly what those finite means might be by which we express infinite thoughts."[6] In other words, there is an odd fact about language that has been apparent for a long time: there are only so many words; yet from these relatively few words one can create (as poets do) an endless variety of nuanced meanings. In fact, there seems to be no end to what can be produced from these limited materials.

It is easy to see how tensions would occur as linguists attempted to map the domain of syntax—a task that proved extremely difficult, as so many different languages exist. How these various maps related to the child's brain and its capacities for generating meaningful sentences and, perhaps, understanding the world in some pre-linguistic fashion, perplexed them. Yet the idea that language differences were superficial remained a primary assumption throughout the last decades of the twentieth century. "The idea was that if you looked more carefully, you could find underlying principles in widely differing languages," Chomsky explained. "If, in fact, we knew the principles used to form and interpret complex (sentence) constructions, at least one major task of linguistics would be solved. It's a scientific question, and a fundamental one, to find out what a person knows without awareness or even possible access to consciousness." In this, linguistics begins to bleed over into other areas of study, including psychology and philosophy.

While the study of language remains an ancient endeavor, going back to Greece and India, there has been consistent philosophical interest in the subject since René Descartes, who is generally considered the founding father of modern philosophy. He noted that the ability to express themselves in words marked "the true distinction" between humans and animals. Language is, then, a property of the species, and unique to it. We are people because we can talk (writing came much later). It is therefore not surprising that there has been consistent, and constantly shifting, speculation about the nature of language itself, its relation to the human mind, and the part it plays in the construction of realities.

The exact nature of poetic language and its relationship to language in general has also been a subject of perpetual debate. Can one really draw a distinction between "poetic" language and the language of prose or ordinary discourse? Traditionally, this discussion usually centers on theories about the origins of language itself, as well as on the question of mimesis, or representation: the relationship between words and things.

In the *Republic,* Plato (in the guise of Socrates, who is often given the best lines) writes about how artists work. Makers of tables and beds, he argues, simply imitate the idea (or ideal form) of such things, whereas the artist has another avenue of approach, that of "turning a mirror round and round."[7] Plato often falls back upon the metaphor of art as a mirror, an analogy that had currency well before he began to use it. One can track this analogy through the Greeks and Romans, who found the comparison useful and stimulating; in fact, Aristotle, Horace, and Longinus each used a version of it in their critical writing about poetry. In the Renaissance, the analogy became a commonplace of criticism. But no analogy, however brilliant, is perfect, in that one thing is not another thing, not *exactly.* My love may be "like a red, red rose," as Robert Burns wrote; but "my love" is not actually a rose. At least, one hopes not.

The mimetic theory of language holds that language mirrors reality; but this is to take a provocative metaphor—language is a mirror—and stretch it. Simonides of Ceos (ca. 556–469 B.C.) was among the first to write about poetry as a mirror, saying that "painting is mute poetry, and poetry a speaking picture." In this widely quoted phrase, sight and sound mingle, which leads naturally to confusion. We can't really speak in pictures, can we? Painting and poetry have something in common, in that they attempt to represent reality in certain intensified ways. Each is synecdochal, too: that is, a little bit of reality stands in for larger parts of reality in most paintings and poems. Yet the comparison soon breaks down. ("A metaphor cannot run on all four legs," Samuel Taylor Coleridge once said.)

In the late eighteenth and early nineteenth centuries in Germany and England, there was a consistent effort to extend or shift the analogy of the mirror, to find other means to describe the relationship between words and things, between language and mind, and to locate the differences between ordinary language and poetic language in the origins of language itself. It was commonly suggested that poetry was the language of emotion, and that this had something to do with the birth of language in the utterances of primitive people, whose speech the Romantics somehow assumed was rhythmical and evocative—like poems. (I suspect that they imagined cave dwellers beating on drums and dancing around a fire.) But this idea as well could be traced back to the ancients, where a good deal of speculation about the origins of language can be found, as when the Roman poet Lucretius suggested that primitive men and women distinguished one thing from another thing by "varying sounds to suit varying feelings." In *De rerum natura* (V) he wrote: "Therefore if different feelings compel animals, dumb though they are, to utter different sounds, how much more natural it is that mortal men should then have been able to mark different things by one sound or another."[8]

Thus language is assumed to have begun in grunts and cries. But how does this relate to poetic language? As M. H. Abrams notes: "The Lucretian theory that language began as a spontaneous expression of feeling was bound sometime to merge with the concurrent belief that the first elaborated form of language was poetic, into the doctrine that poetry preceded prose because poetry is the natural expression of feeling." The notion that poetry arose from emotional states appealed to critics in the eighteenth and nineteenth centuries, especially to those who considered religious emotion the height of feeling. John Dennis, a critic, wrote in 1704, "Religion at first produced [poetry], as a Cause produces its Effect. . . . For the Wonders of Religion naturally threw them upon great Passions, and Great Passions naturally threw them upon Harmony and Figurative Language."[9]

The connection between poetry and religious feeling is (and always has been) deep and consistent; one could in fact argue that spiritual awareness is central to the art itself, and that all poetry aspires to the condition of scripture. This is probably true. But let's draw back a bit, staying with the idea that poetry is simply the expression of emotion—a fairly common assumption among Romantic poets and critics, and one that has trickled down to our time. This notion gives primacy to the lyric as a poetic form, since the lyric represents the direct expression of a feeling. Such a theory obviously downgrades forms of poetry—

including discursive or dramatic poetry—that move away from intensity of expression. Even the traditional epic (a long poem on a heroic theme, such as the founding of a nation) has evaporated in modern times, replaced by the autobiographical epic, such as Wordsworth's *The Prelude* (1850), a poem about "the growth of a poet's mind," or Whitman's *Song of Myself* (1855). While narrative and dramatic poems still interest a number of readers (mostly poets themselves, who enjoy writing them), it will be obvious to anyone who scans an anthology of poetry from the past two centuries that lyric verse dominates the field. Even major long poems, such as *The Waste Land* by T. S. Eliot or *The Cantos* by Ezra Pound, consist of individual lyrics stitched together in some fashion. As John Stuart Mill states rather too baldly, all real poems should be "short poems; it being impossible that a feeling so intense . . . should sustain itself at its highest elevation for long." He also suggests that a long poem will always be felt "to be something unnatural and hollow."[10]

Mill is elaborating on what John Keats suggests, if more obliquely, when he says that "the excellence of every art is its intensity." Applied to poetry, one finds this intensity reflected in the language itself, which separates from ordinary language—the speech used in everyday conversation or in prose—by various means. Thus poetry becomes, in the words of Gerard Manley Hopkins, "the common language heightened." What will vary from poem to poem is the method used to intensify or heighten the language.

It should be obvious, even to the most casual reader, that poetic language relies more heavily on concrete imagery and figures of speech than the language of prose: this accounts for the density of its effects. Poetry also depends on musical qualities that, spread out over paragraphs in prose, would become wearisome and seem peculiar or forced. It is simply not possible to sustain the intensity of poetry for long, just as in life one could never operate at full emotional throttle on a day-to-day basis without burning out. The poem, and its language, draws the senses to a fine point, to a pitch of expression. It involves a level of concentration rarely found in prose. Ideally, it returns us to our deepest concerns, our most intense and original feelings, what Stevens in "Notes Toward a Supreme Fiction" calls "the first idea."

> The poem refreshes life so that we share,
> For a moment, the first idea . . . It satisfies
> Belief in an immaculate beginning
>
> And sends us, winged by an unconscious will,
> To an immaculate end.

. . . . .

Emerson absorbed various Romantic ideas from England and Germany and refigured them in his uniquely aphoristic style, giving them an American expression. There is a brilliant section called "Language" in *Nature* (1836) that still seems entirely relevant and offers a basis for thinking about poetic language in particular. In compressed form, he lays out a useful theory of poetic language; it rests on three principles, which he summarizes as follows:

> Words are signs of natural facts.
> Particular natural facts are symbols of particular spiritual facts.
> Nature is the symbol of spirit.[11]

In the first statement, Emerson plays with the notion that words themselves have buried within them a pictorial content, and that language tends to evolve in the direction of abstractness. In their root meaning, for example, the words *right* and *wrong* mean "straight" and "crooked" and are thus devoid of moral implication. Nevertheless, these extremely concrete words evolved into our most elevated (and portentous) abstractions. The word *transgression* means "crossing the line." The word *supercilious* means "raising an eyebrow." And so on. One could trot happily through the dictionary, returning words again and again to their fresh, concrete, pictorial meanings. Even the word *abstraction* itself contains a picture: *abs* = "away from"; *traction* = "to pull or draw." Hence, the abstraction pulls away from the original concrete picture. The "tractor" of time—in the evolution of the word—yanks the word loose from its original meaning as it suppresses the metaphor.

Poets consistently attempt to return words to their original sense; this is one of the most vivid functions of poetry: to refresh language by drawing words back into alignment with their original pictorial, concrete, and metaphorical associations. One example will do here. In "Design," Robert Frost contemplates a scene of considerable unpleasantness in nature:

> I found a dimpled spider, fat and white,
> On a white heal-all, holding up a moth
> Like a white piece of rigid satin cloth—
> Assorted characters of death and blight
> Mixed ready to begin the morning right,
> Like the ingredients of a witches' broth—

A snow-drop spider, a flower like a froth,
And dead wings carried like a paper kite.

The poet gathers in a single image an unappealing mixture of elements: an albino spider, a dead moth, and a white heal-all (one of the common roadside flowers of New England, which is normally blue). In the sestet of the sonnet, which follows, Frost questions nature itself (or the God behind it), asking three unanswerable questions:

What had that flower to do with being white,
The wayside blue and innocent heal-all?
What brought the kindred spider to that height,
Then steered the white moth thither in the night?
What but design of darkness to appall?—
If design govern in a thing so small.

In other words, what "design" in nature allows for such a terrifying scene? Frost answers his own question slyly: "What but design of darkness to appall?— / If design govern in a thing so small." The emphasis falls on the word *appall*. In its root sense, the word means "to make white." We turn livid (pale) when the blood drains from our cheeks through horror. We are appalled, made white, by scenes of destruction or cruelty or imbalance, as in the scene conjured by Frost. He takes us back to the root of a word that has somehow lost its force through the evolutionary process that leads to abstraction. The poet quickens our sense of language, and our sense of life as well. This is why language matters in a poem, and why poetry matters.

The second idea of Emerson presupposes an almost occult relationship between words and things. "It is not words that are emblematic; it is things which are emblematic. Every natural fact is a symbol of some spiritual fact. Every appearance in nature corresponds to some state of the mind, and that state of the mind can only be described by presenting that natural appearance as its picture." This is to suggest that images embody a state of mind. Certainly many if not most good poems contain images that radiate meaning beyond the most literal level. William Blake in "The Lamb" asks: "Little Lamb, who made thee? / Dost thou know who made thee?" The poem is ostensibly about a lamb, but the reader is aware of the innocence implied. There is poignancy in the poem that owes something to the evocative power of the association itself. But a natural image is always contextual, and so the associations may be manipulated by a poet for certain effects, as in Richard Eberhart's "For a Lamb"—

I saw on the slant hill a putrid lamb,
Propped with daisies. The sleep looked deep,
The face nudged in the green pillow
But the guts were out for crows to eat.

Where's the lamb? whose tender plaint
Said all for the mute breezes.
Say he's in the wind somewhere,
Say, there's a lamb in the daisies.

Eberhart relies on a natural image, but one that dislodges our usual expectations for a lamb, as registered in Blake's poem; here the animal is dead, "putrid," with its "guts . . . out for crows to eat." The reader can draw on the innocence associated with all lambs; but the poet widens the experience, questioning the soul of the lamb, wondering what the "mute breezes" have in mind, with *breezes* being a word associated with the spirit (as in the Latin *spiritus*, meaning "wind" as well as "spirit"). The poem is anything but comforting. The lamb in the daisies draws us back to our own mortality. The image itself is disruptive, with ferocious implications. Yet the language is as fierce as it is simple.

That poets love language is, perhaps, too obvious to say. Words themselves are the raw material of their enterprise. But what poets really love, I think, is what Louise Glück calls "the possibilities of context" in her essay "Education of a Poet." As she says, a poem affords to simple words a circumscribed range of denotation and connotation, a context in which meaning can accumulate, inhere. Glück recalls that, from an early age, she responded to words in a particular linguistic setting. "What I responded to, on the page," she observes, "was the way a poem could liberate, by means of a word's setting, through subtleties of timing, of pacing, that word's full and surprising range of meaning."[12]

Emerson was interested in context as well, and writes interestingly about the juncture of words in relation to the natural world. Words create figures on the page, and these take on meaning *in relation to* their natural context: "Because of this radical correspondence between visible things and human thoughts, savages, who have only what is necessary, converse in figures. As we go back in history, language becomes more picturesque, until its infancy, when it is all poetry; or all spiritual facts are represented by natural symbols." It would be foolish to take Emerson too literally here: I doubt even he believed in some Golden Age of Expression, when primitive men and women walked around speaking a natural poetry. Nevertheless, he rightly observes that the evolution of language from concrete to abstract has moral implications: "The corruption of man is followed by the corruption of language." Old words and their meanings are "perverted," he says. Certainly in political terms one can see that governments and pundits will often use language as a blunt instrument to club their constituencies into imbecility.

In "Politics and the English Language" (1946), George Orwell writes eloquently about the damage that abstraction may cause, suggesting that "a mixture of vagueness and sheer incompetence is the most marked characteristic of modern English prose." This writing consists "less and less of words chosen for the sake of their meaning, and more and more of phrases tacked together like the sections of a prefabricated henhouse." He cites abstraction as the main problem: a dislodging of words from their pictorial origins. Language becomes "prefabricated," a wall of concrete blocks, which are hollow inside. Needless to say, the kind of abstract language Orwell derides lives at the opposite end of the scale from the language of poetry.[13]

Emerson's final point is that nature symbolizes the spirit. "The world is emblematic," he tells us. "Parts of speech are metaphors, because the whole of nature is a metaphor of the human mind." This is a version of Blake's proverbial line from *The Marriage of Heaven and Hell:* "Where man is not, nature is barren." Certainly what invigorates much of the writing of nature poets is the sense of nature as having some connection to the human mind;

it is not a product of the mind, of course. The world has its own reality. But the human imagination makes the world sensible, both literally and figuratively. And the details in nature point to a world of spirit: "All finite things reveal infinitude," as Theodore Roethke writes in "The Far Field." And so, as we ground ourselves in the physical world, we re-ground ourselves in language, which is itself physical. With the help of poetry, we begin to fathom the relations between nature and mind, between matter and spirit.

3 the personal voice

The ear is the only true writer and the only true reader. I have known people who could read without hearing the sentence sounds and they were the fastest readers. Eye readers we call them. They can get the meaning by glances. But they are bad readers because they miss the best part of what a writer puts into his work.

ROBERT FROST

Where shall the scream stick?
What shall it dent?
    Won't the deafness be cracked?
Won't the molecules be loosened?

JORIE GRAHAM

One hears a lot about voice in literary circles, where everyone apparently seeks this valuable commodity, panned for like gold in mountain springs by would-be poets (as well as novelists and others with aspiration to literary quality). But what is this coveted thing? Can it really be defined? How does it relate to the "public voice," the voice of the culture at large, the culture "speaking" itself in the newspapers, on television, in speeches delivered by politicos, and in the very public conversations of pundits and celebrities? To what extent does the usually unheard voice of poetry matter in a world where public and private realms appear always in conflict, where mass culture threatens to overwhelm the personal voice of the poet with its big-throated booming?

It is probably not fruitful to talk about voice in poetry outside the context of particular poets, even particular poems. Four poets in particular—Yeats, Frost, Stevens, and Eliot, perhaps the dominant poetic voices of the first half of the twentieth century—each found a personal voice of considerable range and power. They explored the issue of voice in ways that remain instructive, and their struggles to find a way of writing that was individually true yet somehow representative, even useful in the creation of culture, are worth considering.

Voice remains a difficult concept, somehow akin to literary style, and often aligned with "personality" in writing. Critics look about for ways to discuss it, though much of the literature on this subject remains unhelpful and vague. A typical approach will be found in *The Writer's Idea Book* (2000), in which Jack Heffron attempts to corral a meaning for voice by suggesting that it "is closely related to tone." Heffron suggests that "tone has a bit more to do with what you say; voice has more to do with how you say it." Addressing beginning writers, he suggests that if they continue to work hard, writing poem after poem with dedication and serious application, the "writer's voice will shine through."[1] This is pretty simplistic stuff, wholly inadequate, yet very much the kind of rudimentary talk about voice one hears in poetry workshops. It points up the grave difficulties we have with understanding the notion of voice.

On a more sophisticated level one encounters theorists like Peter Elbow, whose *Writing with Power* (1981) has become a classic for teachers of writing. Elbow sweats at defining voice, admitting how difficult the task is, and creates three categories. In the first grouping will be found texts that have no voice at all: professional writing, textbooks, memos, guidebooks, instruction manuals. I would add newspaper stories to this list, writing where "objectivity" is much prized and in which the illusion of objectivity hides the necessarily subjective viewpoint of the author. To a degree, the public voice (if such a thing exists) would operate in this first category, since this voice is anything but personal, having been scrubbed clean of individuality. As Orwell noted, a great deal of prose falls into the category of clichéd, "prefabricated" language, as writers rely too heavily on stock phrases and abstractions. Prefab language belongs to Elbow's first category.[2]

Into the second category fall those texts that display some degree of personal voice, which Elbow fails to define with precision. This kind of language is a halfway house of sorts, "what most people have in their speech but lack in their writing—namely, a sound or texture—the smell of 'them.'" Elbow may be right or wrong about how much individuality people have in their common speech, but this remains a familiar notion, one developed at length by Robert Frost in his famous discussions of "the sound of sense." He first articulated this idea when writing from England to John Bartlett, a former student: "Now it is possible to have sense without the sound of sense (as in much prose that is supposed to pass muster but makes very dull reading) and the sound of sense without sense (as in *Alice in Wonderland,* which makes anything but dull reading). The best place to get the abstract sound of sense is from voices behind a door that cuts off the words."[3]

Frost equates voice in its most personal aspect with the sound of sense, the patterning of the individual voice, as when you hear someone talking behind a door and know the speaker by the way he or she hangs words together, even without seeing the person or hearing enough of the tone to identify the speaker. Voiceprint, as something self-identifying about a speaking voice, creates the sound of sense. It operates in the second or, ideally, the third category of Elbow's definition, which is the province of "real voice." This is writing with "power and resonance." It is the essence of good writing for Elbow, and what he believes all instructors should attempt to cultivate in their students. It is clearly the realm where genuine poetry occurs.

We live in an age of identity politics, in which marginalized groups—women, gays, immigrant communities, or racial minorities of one kind or another—struggle to "find a voice." Voice connects to power in this regard, and so good writers from the margins are eagerly sought after. Postcolonial theory is a body of recent critical thinking that meditates on the effects of empire and empire building, and on how the impulse to dominate other people works itself out in literary texts. In this theory, we find many discussions of "writing back" and "hybridity" (this latter term refers to the mixing of cultures), and so literary identity and cultural power touch in vital ways, at least in the theory of voice in relation to cultural influence. In these terms, voice often takes the form of political critique, and the voice of the individual writer stands in for the voice of a marginalized group. That is, the writer "writes back" to those in charge, to the oppressor. Unfortunately, the individual is often lost in all of this, as the poet or novelist who "writes back" must represent his or her group at all costs. And so voice becomes an aspect of group definition.[4]

The group-defining voice of such writers stands oddly in contrast to traditional or folk poetry, which is public by definition and therefore devoid of individuality in the modern sense, where voice is the stamp of personality. The fierce requirements of inherited forms (such as the ballad) militate against individual style, although they do not preclude it. Folk poetry usually has a depersonalized aura, an air of anonymity, as if written by society at large, as in the Homeric epics, where the name of Homer perhaps represents many authors and is acknowledged as a fiction, a way of assigning authorship to a poem that belongs to the public, not an individual creator. The same may be said for the book of Psalms, a collection of lyrics by a number of ancient Hebrew poets. The psalms adhere to a somewhat formulaic style that tends to dampen the sense of a personal voice.

In modern and contemporary British and American poetry, the individual voice matters a great deal, and one could not imagine poems by (for example) Ted Hughes or Sylvia Plath composed anonymously. In entrepreneurial cultures, ownership counts. The reader has grown accustomed to locating an individual, to connecting a poem to a poet's life story. In fact, modern poetry after Wordsworth's *The Prelude* tends to be overtly autobiographical, describing the growth of the poet's mind. And not *any* poet's mind. One begins to recognize the voice of a single author. It becomes almost a brand, although that puts it crudely and undermines the genuine achievement of voice in these poets. In contemporary poetry, voice remains important, and one hears the individual note in a wide range of poets whose voices have their own tonal range, their own obsessive subjects, a unique understanding of the work of poetry in relation to the culture at large. In some cases (Seamus Heaney would be an example here) there is an individual diction as well, often derived from a certain geographical area.

There is even a good deal of voice in the so-called L=A=N=G=U=A=G=E poets, such as Charles Bernstein,

Michael Palmer, and Susan Howe, who have struggled mightily to erase this element from their work in order to allow the language itself (and the culture, in a broad sense) to rise into the foreground. Yet even in this poetry, the poets stumble into voice, as the lines develop and poems become pieces of shaped, linguistic reality. Ironies arise here, of course, and in "The Republic of Reality," Bernstein grapples with these, especially in the poignant concluding section, where the poet writes lines about lines, trying to understand how the voice in the line relates (or doesn't) to the reality it attempts to represent, embody, reflect, or—in this case—deflect:

> This line is stripped of emotion.
> This line is no more than an
> illustration of a European
> theory. This line is bereft
> of a subject. This line
> has no reference apart
> from its context in
> this line. This line
> is only about itself.
> This line has no meaning:
> its words are imaginary, its
> sounds inaudible. This line
> cares not for itself or for
> anyone else—it is indifferent,
> impersonal, cold, uninviting.
> This line is elitist, requiring,
> to understand it, years of study
> over esoteric treatises on
> impossible to pronounce topics.
> This line refuses reality.

. . . . .

The modernists wrestled furiously with the issue of voice in relation to poetic language, often trying to write themselves out of their work, deflecting attention from the poetic "I" to language itself, to the voice of history. *The Waste Land* would have to be seen as a primary attempt to allow history to speak for itself, if such a thing can be done. The many voices of that poem, and the endless quotations from earlier poems, work effectively to create a distinct sound, if not actually a voice. That sound or poetic note is despairing, cynical, and fragmentary. But Eliot worked in the shadow of Yeats, the primary poet in the English language when he began to write.

By the early twentieth century, Yeats had established himself as a poet at once marginal (Irish, revolutionary) and central (appropriating all the dominant forms of English poetry, mastering blank verse, myriad stanza forms, traditional symbols, and so forth). He began as a poet of the Celtic Revival, cloaking himself in ancient Irish mythology and Irish history. He soon invented a series of ingenious masks for himself, such as Michael Robartes or Owen Aherne, the former representing his more mystical side, the latter his political self. (These masks are set in dialogue in "The Phases of the Moon," one of his most vivid poems.) These masks allowed him to discover a voice, or many voices, rather indirectly.

The notion of the mask itself is the subject of "The Mask," a dialogue in which Yeats contemplates the use of personae as part of a quest for authenticity:

"Put off that mask of burning gold
With emerald eyes."

"O no, my dear, you make so bold
To find if hearts be wild and wise,
And yet not cold."

"I would but find what's there to find,
Love or deceit."
"It was the mask engaged your mind,
And after set your heart to beat,
Not what's behind."

"But lest you are my enemy,
I must enquire."
"O no, my dear, let all that be;
What matter, so there is but fire
In you, in me?"

In his early years as poet, Yeats wore many masks. He did so literally as well, as a leading member of the Hermetic Students of the Golden Dawn, a quasi-mystical group committed to arcane ceremonies. More figuratively, he put on the mask of Irish revolutionary during the early decades of the century, in part to please Maud Gonne, a revolutionary leader whom he loved, without much luck (at least in the romantic sense). He also wore the masks of lover and seer (or Blakean mystic). Whether (as the above poem suggests) there is "love or deceit" behind these various masks becomes an irrelevancy, so long as there is fire in the speaker. That is, so long as the mask functions as a means to organize and convey feelings, to represent a passionate point of view.

For Yeats, a mask was related to what he called the "antithetical" self. In his diary, he wrote: "I think all happiness depends on having the energy to assume the mask of some other self; that all joyous or creative life is a rebirth as something not oneself—

something created in a moment and perpetually renewed; in playing a game like that of a child where one loses the infinite pain of self-realization, a grotesque or solemn painted face put on that one may haste from the terrors of judgement."[5] In other words, art takes one beyond self-expression. It moves toward the realization of new selves. For Yeats, there is never a single "self" identified with a person; instead, masks reflect the reality of multiple, even antithetical, selves.

It will be worth thinking about "personality" here, a word commonly tossed around but little understood. The word *person* derives from the Latin *persona,* which may be defined as *per sona,* "the voice sounding through [the mask]." To an extent, there is no such thing as a maskless face; one assumes a point of view, an angle, a tone, a color. In all writing, the author must self-authorize: create his or her own mask and peer through the eye-holes. The voice that emerges is given shape and substance by the contours of the mask, which fits well or doesn't, although in time a mask may come to fit, as the face grows into its contours, becomes identified with the speaker. It can even prove difficult to remove an unpleasant, uncongenial mask, one that comes to feel distinctly inauthentic. This conflict lies at the core of the dialogue between self and soul that preoccupied Yeats as a poet for many decades.

Critics often prefer the later poems of Yeats to the earlier ones, in which his masks were more artificial and the personal voice seemed deflected or inflated. A turning point in his career came with "A Coat," a little gem wherein he casts off the elaborate masks of his early verse, characterized by the poet as a coat "Covered with embroideries / Out of old mythologies / From heel to throat." He proposes to walk naked now, without a mask, as if that were possible.

Certainly a personal voice emerges in the later poems that seems less artificial, less vigorously constructed, than that in the earlier work. Paradoxically, it also seems like a more public voice, as in "Among School Children," where Yeats stands in propria persona (in his own person, that is, as himself)—"a sixty-year-old smiling public man" gently mocking his own mask as senator of the Irish Free State (he served from 1922 to 1928 in this capacity). By the last decades of his life Yeats had become the master of his masks, slipping them off and on with ease, often contemplating the bizarre range of faces he deployed, as in "The Circus Animals' Desertion," where he recollects old selves, old masks, old mythologies, and proposes to put everything aside, to let those circus animals—tamed creatures all—run wild. He proposes to lie down "in the foul rag-and-bone shop of the heart."

That poem begins with a crisis of inspiration, as the poet talks about having sought a theme for some six weeks without locating one:

I sought a theme and sought for it in vain,
I sought it daily for six weeks or so.
Maybe at last, being but a broken man,
I must be satisfied with my heart, although
Winter and summer till old age began
My circus animals were all on show,
Those stilted boys, that burnished chariot,
Lion and woman and the Lord knows what.

Urgency and frankness can be heard in these lines, so free of cant, so wildly personal. Old age brought Yeats to the brink of a new simplicity, and the poems of his last books shimmer with the radiance of this grace. This may have been, of course, the final mask, but it fits very well, and its shape seems to adhere snugly to the shape of the imagined face.

Robert Frost adored Yeats from the beginning of his career, when he was a poultry farmer and teacher in New Hampshire. Indeed, he directed two of Yeats's verse plays, *The Land of Heart's Desire* and *Cathleen ni Houlihan,* while teaching at the Pinkerton Academy in 1910. He actually met Yeats while living in England in the years just prior to the outbreak of the Great War, and he took a good deal of interest in the idea of the mask. Frost develops a variety of masks in *North of Boston* (1914), his second book, in which he perfects a kind of dramatic poetry that is very much his own. The rustic New England farmers who populate these poems are self-consciously devised personae. They are not the stuff of old mythologies; rather, Frost looks around him, plucking characters from the landscapes of rural New Hampshire or Vermont, where most of these poems are set. One thinks of Mary and Warren in "Death of a Hired Man," each so distinctly realized, and each so perfectly Frost. Or Lafe, Magoon, and the night clerk in "A Hundred Collars." Or the benighted couple who have recently buried a child (as did the Frosts) in "Home Burial." These are just a few of the many distinct figures who appear in these poems, and later ones as well, such as the despairing hill wife of the poem by that name, or Coles and Meserve in "Snow," or any of the rueful, proud, stubborn figures who speak up in *New Hampshire* and later books. Indeed, Frost never ceased to use personae, writing dramatic poems such as *A Masque of Reason* and *A Masque of Mercy* in the mid-1940s.

Frost uses masks not to deflect the personal voice but to find one, or several. He speaks truthfully when speaking as someone else, when he can assume the otherness of a mask, looking through those eyeholes at the world. Tone, he notes, is how you take yourself, your stance toward the world; literally, it is your attitude. Paradoxically, it seems harder to speak as one's self without the sustained practice of speaking as somebody else. But Frost did use many voices, so that when he speaks in the lyric "I" of, say, "The Road Not Taken," he does so with a sense of well-earned authenticity, as in the canny final stanza, where the "sigh" of the speaker acknowledges the mask of the wise old man who looks back and pretends that one path was different from the other, even though he has spent much of the poem explaining there was no difference at all between them:

> I shall be telling this with a sigh
> Somewhere ages and ages hence:
> Two roads diverged in a wood, and I—
> I took the road less traveled by,
> And that has made all the difference.

By the time Frost composed this ingenious, sly poem, he had practiced himself in different voices for many years, and found what felt right and true. Of course, Frost was inventing himself, using a mask, even when speaking supposedly as himself. One must *never* confuse the "I" of a lyric poem with the poet; the "I" is just an eye, or two eyeholes poked through a makeshift construction. But if Frost sounds remarkably fresh, colloquial, and authentic in his lyric poems, this has much to do with being acquainted with otherness by having tried on so many guises, by having worn the antithetical uniform of other selves self-consciously, even bravely. He learned how to speak in another's voice so that in those moments of sublime self-revelation one covets in literary texts, he could speak as himself as well. When, in old age, he stepped onto countless public platforms and wore the mask of the old, wise, weather-beaten farmer-poet, he did so having explored a variety of masks over many decades; he felt comfortable in the end with that one, and wore it well. It even seemed, toward the end, a true representation, about as comfortable as any mask could ever get for a man as guarded and ambivalent as Robert Frost.[6]

Another of the massive figures who brought a distinctly personal voice to modern poetry was Wallace Stevens. He did so by writing mostly in a highly individual version of Romantic blank verse, an idiom with roots in Miltonic blank verse (as in *Paradise Lost,* with its propulsive sense of argument as the lines tumble over themselves, accumulating force over many lines, even whole sections) but filtered through *The Prelude,* where Wordsworth was able to retain an aura of sublimity without overreaching, keeping a personal note in the blank verse—which is no mean feat, as the form itself often seems to eat into the individuality of the poet. The personal voice of *The Prelude* may well be regarded as the guiding voice of modern poetry. It was a medium, or voice, that deftly combined a public stance with an intensely private sensibility. Fostered alike "by beauty and by fear," Wordsworth knew exactly how to create a rhetoric that bridged the realms of ordinary discourse and intense self-exploration as he tracked the growth of a poet's mind over many years. That confessional element was new in poetry, with its freshness, candor, and almost indecent inwardness. Of course this was a fiction, as the lyric voice in poetry is always a "made thing," shaped from various public and private materials. But Wordsworth thrived on self-revelation.

Stevens did not. He ranks among the least autobiographical of poets, one who takes poetry itself—in the broadest sense, representing all constructions—as his subject. His apprenticeship was slow and careful. Indeed, he waited until middle age to publish his first volume, and when *Harmonium* finally appeared, in 1923, it contained multitudes of voice-prints. In this capacious volume, Stevens tries on many personae, some of them flamboyant. Only in rare instances does an accent that could remotely be called personal appear. Even "Sunday Morning," one of his finest early poems, seems oddly impersonal, even in the glorious last stanza, with its succulent evocation of reality, the "old chaos of the sun," where deer walk upon the mountain, sweet berries ripen in the wilderness, and those ambiguous pigeons sink "downward to darkness, on extended wings."

Stevens dons mask after mask, as in "The Comedian as the Letter C," where he writes as Crispin, the sensualist and aesthete:

> Crispin at sea
> Created, in his day, a touch of doubt.
> An eye most apt in gelatines and jupes,
> Berries of villages, a barber's eye,
> An eye of land, of simple salad-beds,
> Of honest quilts, the eye of Crispin, hung
> On porpoises, instead of apricots,
> And on silentious porpoises, whose snouts
> Dibbled in waves that were mustachios,
> Inscrutable hair in an inscrutable world.

The language here is difficult: intensely wrought, artificial in the extreme, baroque in affect. This is far from Gerard Manley Hopkins's definition of poetry as "the common language *heightened*." Heightened is one thing, strung up another. I have a difficult time with Stevens at his most baroque, although he backs off these excesses in such lovely early poems as "The Snow Man," "The Idea of Order at Key West," or "Anecdote of a Jar."

Throughout his long career, Stevens moved in and out of personae, whether writing as Crispin or Canon Aspirin (in "Notes Toward a Supreme Fiction") or, more grandly, as Central Man, a figure derived from Whitman, who believed that when a poet writes most truly, he or she writes most representatively, standing in for the reader, for everyone. There is truth in this, although it must live within the paradox of personal speech becoming public speech: exactly what happens in *The Prelude,* in *Song of Myself,* in "Sunday Morning," in "Notes Toward a Supreme Fiction," and in the last, bare poems of *The Rock,* where, stripped of mask and damask, Stevens takes off the burning gold and looks at the reader directly, unmasking himself as he unmasks the reader.

I can think of no more affecting poem than "Final Soliloquy of the Interior Paramour," a kind of secular psalm, a hymn to human possibilities within the folds of imagination and grace. This is, as Stevens says elsewhere, a "poem of the mind / In the act of finding what will suffice." In the sphere of this poem, the listener is told to "think / The world imagined is the ultimate good." As always, in the late Romantic tradition that Stevens upholds, the secondary imagination (as described by Coleridge) is that which breaks apart the "real" world, reconstitutes it. In this reformed world, it remains possible to believe in the purity of truly imagined reality. "We say God and the imagination are one," Stevens propounds. He proclaims this equivalence, in any case, and it is sufficient in his mouth.

"Ariel was glad he had written his poems," Stevens suggests in a late poem, "The Planet on the Table." The sun in Stevens always represents reality, the "old chaos of the sun," a reality unmodified by the imagination. But toward the end there is a self-sufficiency that is very touching: "His self and the sun were one / And his poems, although makings of his self, / Were no less makings of the sun." The deepest self is identified here with reality, with the white-hot center of the sun; to this the imagination adds what it can. The gaudy masks worn by Stevens in earlier years give way to a plain sense of things, to a voice remarkable in its purity and bareness, its refusal to adorn reality with gold or gold enamellings, as Yeats would have said. The masks fall away, and what is left is a strong but hardly elaborate or overwrought voice. This voice is the "scrawny cry" heard in March and described in the last poem in Stevens's *Collected Poems,* "Not

Ideas About the Thing but the Thing Itself." This voice is "part of the colossal sun," he says. "It was like / A new knowledge of reality."

The achievement of late Stevens is the attainment of a personal note, embodying a "new knowledge of reality." The poet acquires this inestimable knowledge by having moved through the unimagined, unimaginable winter of "The Snow Man," through the endless theatrical selves that speak through masks in the poems of his early and middle years, back to reality again. That final reality is, of course, modified, informed, and reformulated by the poet, whose voice has evolved, as he says in this final poem, beyond the "vast ventriloquism" that had occupied him for so long, as he spoke through more elaborate personae.

Finally, I return to Eliot, who was aptly called "the invisible poet" by Hugh Kenner. It is not easy to locate Eliot himself in his early to middle years. In his first incarnation as poet he speaks through the mask of J. Alfred Prufrock—a fussy, self-conscious and self-denigrating figure who might have fit comfortably into a novel by Henry James. Eliot is doubtless mocking himself on some level by assuming a name not unlike the names he had used upon his arrival in England, where he signed himself variously as T. Stearns-Eliot or Thomas S. Eliot or Tom, plain Tom, whom his friend Ezra Pound referred to as Possum, the poet who preferred to hide behind any number of guises.

The Waste Land (1922) was originally called "He Do the Police in Different Voices," after a character in Dickens who imitated various policemen. It is a poem of many voices, none of them identifiable as Eliot himself. The very referentiality of the poem, its endless allusion to other texts, militates against the personal voice. Eliot summons, arranges in deft juxtaposition, a vast anthology of voices, none of them Eliot's as such—or they are Eliot speaking through Baudelaire, Wagner, Ezekiel, Dante, Virgil, Saint Augustine, Spenser, and so forth. The poem is a living testament to the myth of Babel, and Eliot becomes a version of Stevens's great ventriloquist, hiding behind myriad figures, coyly, cleverly, compulsively.

The Waste Land speaks, as I suggest above, as the voice of history itself. It is an avowedly public poem, one that somehow manages, through different voices, to sound like its age. The mournfulness of the postwar era lives here, with its ennui, its ferocious gloom, its despair, its wry cynicism. Like the bird in Yeats's "Sailing to Byzantium" who perches upon a golden bough to sing of what is past or passing or to come, Eliot's primary mask, that of Tiresias, has seen everything, being part Hermes, part Aphrodite: the hermaphrodite who understands life from both sides of the great divide. He is, Eliot claims (in his footnote to line 218), "the most important personage in the poem, uniting all the rest." He sees "the substance of the poem." In a sense, Tiresias is Eliot himself, the voice sounding through all the different masks.

Not until *Four Quartets* (1943) did Eliot let himself speak in the most intimate way. In many ways, I don't really hear Eliot in a self-consciously personal mode until "East Coker," where he writes:

So here I am, in the middle way, having had twenty years—
Twenty years largely wasted, the years of *l'entre deux guerres*—

Trying to learn to use words, and every attempt
Is a wholly new start, and a different kind of failure
Because one has only learnt to get the better of words
For the thing one no longer has to say, or the way in which
One is no longer disposed to say it.

Such a note is rare in Eliot, although it emerges periodically throughout the *Quartets,* his most personal work (which I explore in detail in Chapter 9). Eliot seems not to need elaborate masks in this meditative sequence, where he writes, not unlike Stevens at the end, with a newfound simplicity and openness, an apparent lack of artifice. Of course, even in the above passage, the "middle way" summons the figure of Dante, from the famous opening lines of the *Inferno.* And the "I" of Eliot quickly fades into the less personal "one" who can't get the better of words except for something he no longer wishes to say or in a way he is no longer disposed to say it.

The major modern poets—Yeats, Frost, Stevens, and Eliot—struggled to find a voice (or voices) with enough gravity to weigh in suitably in the first decades of the twentieth century—a period of immense stress, when the world seemed to be coming apart, and where individuality itself seemed threatened by various mass movements and from mass culture itself, which had suddenly so many more powerful outlets for its depersonalized voice. These poets had to fight their way toward personal expression, ducking behind this or that guise, aware that self-consciously taking on masks becomes a useful way to experiment with voice. They all seem to have understood that personality is an invention as much as a discovery, and that a personal voice is only achieved self-consciously, over the long haul, by sounding through mouth holes not necessarily their own, by looking through eye-holes that hide their glittering, emerald eyes. A mask shapes the voice, gives it tone and color, makes it real, so that in the end one can agree with the speaker in Yeats's poem: "'It was the mask engaged your mind, / And after set your heart to beat, / Not what's behind.'"

Although easily recognized, voice eludes easy definition. It gathers in the words and syntax, the tone, of the poet who has worked hard and listened long. It is always a marvelous thing to apprehend, pulsing softly against the abstract and prefabricated voice of the culture at large, which bangs away in our ears throughout the day. In this way, poetry offers an antidote to the bludgeoning loud voices of mass culture, insisting on the still, small voice, the personal voice, thus staking a claim for what used to be called the individual soul.

4 the way of metaphor

I have wanted in late years to go further and further in making metaphor the whole of thinking.

ROBERT FROST

There is always an analogy between nature and the imagination and possibly poetry is merely the strange rhetoric of that parallel: a rhetoric in which the feeling of one man is communicated to another in words of the exquisite appositeness that takes away all their verbality.

WALLACE STEVENS

There is a soul in me
It is asking
to be given its body

LOUISE GLÜCK

P oetry could easily be called the language of metaphor, that
figure of speech which offers a way of seeing one thing in
terms of another. Poetry feasts on the similarities and dif-
ferences between things. Indeed, a poet might well be described
(in Aristotle's terms) as someone capable of noticing likenesses.
Exactly how metaphor works in poetry, and why this matters,
will be the subject of this chapter.

As suggested in the chapter epigraph, Frost was obsessed by
metaphor, and by all forms of analogical thought, including his
favorite figure of speech, synecdoche, whereby the part stands in
for the whole (as when someone says, "Let's count noses"). Most
poets share his obsession and understand in a visceral way that it
matters how we use metaphors. Frost argued strenuously that a
proper understanding of the dynamics of metaphorical thought
was the mark of an educated mind. In "Education by Poetry,"
he goes so far as to suggest that "unless you are at home in the
metaphor, you are not safe anywhere. Because you are not at ease
with figurative values: you don't know the metaphor in its strength
and its weakness. You don't know how far you may expect to ride
it and when it may break down with you. You are not safe in sci-
ence; you are not safe in history."[1] This is a huge claim, yet one I
would stand by. Science and history rest fundamentally on count-

less analogies, and without some objective appreciation of the effects and transformations of metaphor, we risk misunderstandings, which in certain circumstances can be dangerous. (One might, for example, examine the phrase "war on terror" as an implicit metaphor in need of serious deconstruction.)

Stevens was another obsessive proponent of metaphorical thinking. In a lovely essay called "Effects of Analogy," he writes that poetry "is a transcendent analogue composed of the particulars of reality." Like Frost, he took metaphorical thought to its farthest edge, always contemplating the relationship between reality and the imagination. For him, metaphor mediated that relationship. And the word *poetry* itself, in his verse, stands in for this "transcendent analogue" overall. It represents human thought at its highest pitch in its ability to make associations and connections and, indeed, substitutions, as when Shakespeare's Romeo says, "Juliet is the sun," in *Romeo and Juliet* (II, ii).[2]

A good deal of theoretical work has been done on metaphor, beginning with Aristotle's *Poetics*. Many of the best minds of classical Rome, including Cicero and Quintilian, took up the subject as part of their larger discussion of rhetoric. Roman ideas about figures of speech (which often depend on metaphor) became elaborate, often confusing. Indeed, Quintilian threw up his arms in despair, noting the profusion of divisions and subdivisions among different kinds of analogical figures. During the Middle Ages, a period dominated by theological matters, allegory and symbol took on religious significance, and rhetoricians carefully examined the various layers of significance that a text might contain. In the Renaissance, an era when the learning of the ancient poets and philosophers became suddenly available and interesting again, Julius Scaliger developed an elaborate theory of metaphor in his *Poetices libri septem* (1561), in which he examines metaphor in relation to other rhetorical figures in mind-boggling detail. German, French, and English critics of the eighteenth and nineteenth centuries also wrote a good deal about metaphor, which became the bedrock of Romantic theory, and the twentieth century was rife with theoreticians in the field, including (most recently) Umberto Eco, Nelson Goodman, and George Lakoff and Mark Johnson. A fascinating survey of this complex and sometimes difficult terrain can be found in Miriam Taverniers's *Metaphor and Metaphorology* (2002), which offers a selective genealogy of metaphor as a concept from Aristotle to the turn of the twenty-first century.[3]

"Metaphor is the application to one thing of the name belonging to another," says Aristotle in his *Poetics*.[4] The word itself derives from *metapheron,* a Greek term referring to the "carrying over" of meaning from one word to another, much as the word *translation* (*trans-latus*) suggests a carrying over of meaning from one language to another. One thing is not another thing, as Aristotle notes; but in the alchemy of metaphor a kind of substitution occurs, and so "Juliet is the sun." Or "My love is like a red, red rose," as Robert Burns proclaimed.

Let's make a simple metaphor from the above simile by Burns: "My love is a rose." "My love" is the first term, often called the *tenor* (in terminology developed by I. A. Richards in the 1930s); "a rose" is the second term, also called the *vehicle* (by Richards).

George Lakoff (a linguist who has contributed importantly in recent years to the theory of metaphor) refers to these terms as *target* and *source*. Linguists often refer to *ground* and *tension* when talking about metaphor, the ground being the tenor, and the tension referring to the areas of similarity and—perhaps more important—the areas of difference, where the metaphor fails to connect or connects in tangential or complicating ways.[5]

The varieties of metaphorical thinking extend to a range of analogical concepts, including such tropes or figures of speech as simile, conceit, allegory, metonymy, and synecdoche. In each of these things, comparisons are made, implicitly or explicitly. What linguists such as Lakoff and Johnson have suggested, brilliantly, is that metaphors are more than merely decorative, as classical rhetoricians seemed to imply. Rather, metaphor is the fiber of language itself. As such, analogical thinking is central to the human enterprise of making sense. It actually organizes our experience in subtle ways. Without metaphor, there is no thinking at all.

It was Emerson who pointed out that every word was once a metaphor. And so poets often dig into the language like archaeologists, excavating in the soil and subsoil of diction, reclaiming the concreteness and metaphorical freshness of terms. But one could go further here, looking (as Lakoff and Johnson do) at the metaphorical aspects of language as a whole: as in my above phrase, "metaphor is the fiber of language itself." The implicit metaphor here, somewhat hidden (like most metaphors), is that language is like a piece of material, perhaps a cord or cloth. Such metaphors actually direct our thinking, playing an active role in the creation of meaning. In the past decades, as poststructural theories such as deconstruction, feminism, and New Historicism have enlarged (and sometimes distorted) our sense of how literary texts function, there has been considerable attention paid to metaphor. Jacques Derrida (one of the founders of deconstruction) regarded language as an endless chain of signifiers that cannot easily be closed off; it therefore becomes difficult to distinguish between the literal and figurative aspects of language. So ideology (which is subjective) plays a huge role in validating certain interpretations and undermining others.[6]

Poetry matters because it helps us to comprehend metaphor and its extended family of concepts, such as synecdoche. Poets employ various types of analogical thinking. But they understand that a comparison breaks down at some point, and they test the strength of comparisons in their poems, going as far as they can go out on a limb until the limb itself will bear no more: hence, Frost's idea in "Education by Poetry" that one must know how far to go, and how far not to go, in striking analogies. This is thinking itself, and poetry—as a form of figural thought—refines our ability to work within the limits of metaphor and to benefit from its awesome resources.

Metaphors, under certain circumstances, become symbols, and it is worth looking briefly at the "progress" from metaphor and simile to symbol that may occur. A simile is an acknowledged metaphor, as in "My love is like a red, red rose." With a simile, one senses a slight falling off in confidence from a direct metaphor, as in "Juliet is the sun"—a vastly bolder comparison. Simile acknowledges the metaphor while backing away from it, allowing more tension to occur between the vehicle and the tenor (or ground). Burns, who rarely takes poetical thinking to any height, quickly abandons his rose simile and moves on to comparing his love to a "melody" that is "sweetly played in tune." In other words, he wants out quickly. Poets will often, however, move from metaphor or simile to symbol.

But what is a symbol exactly?

On its most basic level, a symbol is anything that stands in for something else. It is a kind of metaphor, although it derives its full strength from a range of associations, which may be traditional or personal, conscious or unconscious. When Dante as pilgrim, at the end of the *Paradiso,* approaches God, he first encounters the rose of paradise, a traditional symbol of wholeness and perfection. In "To the Rose upon the Rood of Time," Yeats gathers this flower to himself at the outset of the poem, hoping to elicit from readers a familiar array of thoughts: "Red Rose, proud Rose, sad Rose of all my days! / Come near me, while I sing the ancient ways." Yeats himself glosses this poem, writing about the rose as "for many centuries a symbol of spiritual love and supreme beauty." It is also "a principal symbol of the divine nature, and the symbolic heart of things." He tells us that it is "the flower sacred to the Virgin Mary" as well as "the western Flower of Life." It may also be considered "a symbol of woman's beauty." Yeats himself recalls in a commentary on this poem that the ancient Celts considered the rose a symbol of Old Ireland.[7]

As one can see, the range of association in Yeats's mind was large and extended in various directions, sacred and profane.

Let's consider the rose in another context, "The Sick Rose," by William Blake, a poem that exploits the symbolic nature of the flower in intriguing ways:

O Rose, thou art sick!
The invisible worm
That flies in the night,
In the howling storm,

Has found out thy bed
Of crimson joy,
And his dark secret love
Does thy life destroy.

What kind of rose is this? One can only guess, beginning the process of association and thus bringing all sorts of personal meanings into play as well as the traditional associations, such as those mentioned by Yeats. Many critics in the past half a century have examined this poem, often with wildly different results, ranging from Northrop Frye and Hazard Adams (fairly standard approaches in the manner of the New Criticism, an important school of literary theory that focused on the internal dynamics of the text itself, often without reference to its biographical or sociological contexts) through feminists such as Elizabeth Langland, who sees the poem within the context of the patriarchal system; she finds in the text both "suspicion and possible hostility" toward women. In fact, the poem—as a symbolic presentation—will accommodate all sorts of readings.[8]

A symbol is a comparison in which the vehicle is split off from the tenor. Instead of "My love is like a red, red rose," we simply get the rose—or a sick rose, as in Blake's poem. This rose may stand in for all sorts of things: a woman, a country, a spiritual condition. We have been told that it is sick and therefore not quite itself. The bloom is off the rose, so to speak. Beyond that, we have little knowledge of what has caused the illness. The "invisible worm" that flies through the storm at night is probably male, as Langland suggests, although I must hesitate here. There are critics who believe that anything longer than it is wide must be a phallic symbol. Yet this worm *does* appear phallic, especially as it approaches the "bed" of the feminine rose. It is possessed of a "dark secret love" that may well be erotic; it may also be "dark" because its motives are not wholly admirable. It wants to unmake or "deflower" the rose, perhaps? In any case, it ruins the rose. The rather masturbatory bed of this rose, which seems to enjoy its "crimson joy," has obvious narcissistic overtones. But if Blake was angry with some specific woman, who can say? In any case, she has been "found out" and destroyed.

A symbol is like a stone tossed into a pond. The stone makes a huge splash at first: this is the most immediate level of signification. Concentric rings of meaning radiate from the point of the splash itself. The farthest rings of meaning may bear only the slightest connection to the initial splash, to the stone that hit the water. These far-flung (far-fetched?) interpretations wash up on the shore, where they may or may not be relevant. Some interpretations may be highly personal and subjective, forming a ring of associations that exist only in the head of the reader. There is often some validity in the remotest rings, although sometimes the connection is lost. In a sense, poetry teaches us how far to go, and how far not to go, with an interpretation, as Frost suggests.

One of my favorite contemporary poems is "Messengers" by Louise Glück. The poet works by symbol, opening with a mysterious evocation of messengers embodied in geese and deer, who approach us from the margins, visible in the periphery of our vision at first, then consuming our attention:

> You have only to wait, they will find you.
> These geese flying low over the marsh,
> glittering in black water.
> They find you.
>
> And the deer—
> how beautiful they are,
> as though their bodies did not impede them.
> Slowly they drift into the open
> through bronze panels of sunlight.

But these are messengers. As symbols, the geese and deer appeal to our senses, to our deepest longings. One has to let the unconscious mind absorb these creatures. "You have only to let it happen," says Glück in another line. The poem invites us to look beyond the literal, and to find a responsiveness in the natural world that might otherwise be ignored. The poem continues, adding to the complexity of these images, adding the human eye, which tries to interpret what it sees, "wounded and dominant," trying—sometimes too hard—to master what it perceives.

. . . . .

In "The Motive for Metaphor," Stevens explores analogical think-
ing from a somewhat idiosyncratic but wonderfully suggestive
angle of vision:

> You like it under the trees in autumn,
> Because everything is half dead.
> The wind moves like a cripple among the leaves
> And repeats words without meaning.
>
> In the same way, you were happy in spring,
> With the half colors of quarter-things,
> The slightly brighter sky, the melting clouds,
> The single bird, the obscure moon—
>
> The obscure moon lighting an obscure world
> Of things that would never be quite expressed,
> Where you yourself were never quite yourself
> And did not want nor have to be,
>
> Desiring the exhilarations of changes:
> The motive for metaphor, shrinking from
> The weight of primary noon,
> The A B C of being,
>
> The ruddy temper, the hammer
> Of red and blue, the hard sound—
> Steel against intimation—the sharp flash,
> The vital, arrogant, fatal, dominant X.

The "you" of the poem, who likes it under the trees, catches
the ear of the reader with its oddity. Stevens refers to himself as
"you," although he subtly implicates the reader as well. There is
the sense of direction here: You will like it, or you ought to like
it, under those autumn trees, where "The wind moves like a

cripple among the leaves / And repeats words without meaning."
Stevens posits an Ur-language here, one prior to that which exists in writing or even speaking: syntax without words. This is, perhaps, a form of pure thought. Wind is, in its root sense, *spiritus:* that which fans the soul to a fine flame. But this wind moves "like a cripple." Why do "you" like that? Perhaps the slowness of the wind, its desultory movements, these "words without meaning," trump the stronger (and less comfortable or comforting) winds of reality, which blow elsewhere—in winter, for instance. At least a cripple can still move; a dead person can't.

In Stevens, winter signifies reality (as in his amazing poem "The Snow Man"), whereas summer is the height of imagination. Fall and spring are liminal seasons that reflect the dialectic between reality and imagination that is the subject of so many of his poems, which he calls (in "Notes Toward a Supreme Fiction") that "war between the mind and sky." One can sift through his *Collected Poems* and create two categories, with "reality" on one side and "imagination" on the other. Reality is signified by words like *winter, sun, north, blue.* The imagination attracts opposite words, including *summer, moon, south, green.* In the second and third stanzas above, Stevens prefers the spring, with its "obscure moon lighting an obscure world." He can nestle in that obscurity, and shrink from full self-disclosure, and get away from the harsh glare of absolute being, get away from death itself. He likes "things that would never be quite expressed," that Ur-language of the wind without words. Metaphor allows for the impossible, a world in which one thing is another thing, and so "Juliet is the sun." In this world of metaphorical alchemy, changes occur and they seem true; the poet *makes* them true. Stevens desires, as he says, "the exhilarations of changes." Metaphor represents metamorphosis.

The changing world of analogy stands in contrast to the harsh glare of reality, where nothing changes, as in death. Stevens thinks of this world as being without nuance (perhaps like the hearty types who played football at Harvard, with their ruddy cheeks aglow?), represented here as the "ruddy temper." He sees reality as the hammer that hits the anvil, rings and flashes. This is vital stuff, of course, but also arrogant and fatal. The poet seems to prefer something less vital, less arrogant, perhaps less fatal: the exhilarating shift of meaning that occurs as one thing is carried over, becoming another thing. This is a world of changes, and the world of poetry, where one thing becomes another thing and where language itself achieves—to quote Stevens —such an "exquisite appositeness" with reality so profound that it "takes away all verbality." So we return again to words without meaning, lifted by the winds, laid bare.

5 tradition and originality

Some writers confuse authenticity,
which they ought always to aim at,
with originality, which they should
never bother about.

W. H. AUDEN

The fact is that every writer creates
his own precursors. His work
modifies our conception of the
past, as it will modify the future.

JORGE LUIS BORGES

I need a virgin mirror
no one's ever looked at,
that's never looked back at anyone,
to flash up the spirits' eyes
and help me recognize them.

ELIZABETH BISHOP

Tradition, that much-abused term, is often set in opposition to what T. S. Eliot called "the individual talent." How poets deal with tradition and with what the critic W. Jackson Bate referred to as "the burden of the past" or what Harold Bloom, a leading contemporary theorist of literary tradition and its effects, termed "the anxiety of influence" has been widely debated. Perhaps too much has been made of this burden or anxiety—poets have always contended with the great figures who went before them, and they have usually done so by reinventing them in their own way, taking what they need as they require it, discarding what is no longer of use. Only ignorance of the past condemns them to mindless repetition, and that is unlikely to happen with serious writers, as all writing begins—and ends—with reading.

Poetry is "about" the past, in that poets understand that language itself is history and that words have slipped through time, undergone mutations, shifts of meaning; but each word is a palimpsest as well: it contains multiple erasures, which underlie its current meaning, coloring it, giving it character and ambiguity and direction. A poem, in this sense, is also a palimpsest, a "writing over" of previous poems, and therefore a gift to the future, where it will be misread, misdirected, even misplaced.

But the strong poem never goes away entirely. It survives, as W. H. Auden says in his elegy for Yeats, in "the valley of its making." In the best circumstances, the poem becomes a valley itself, and the waters of its language follow a course to the sea.

Eliot had an acute sense of the past and its relevance for writers. In his seminal essay "Tradition and the Individual Talent," he put in place some key formulations about the relation between past and present, and these have governed discussions of this subject for much of the past century. For Eliot, the literary past (what is now commonly referred to as the canon) is a living organism, not a static catalogue of works. The past exerts pressure on the present, even helps to determine its nature and direction; what Eliot noticed was that the present also exerts an influence on the past. That is, whenever a new work of art is introduced, it modifies our sense of the order of past works: "The existing monuments form an ideal order among themselves, which is modified by the introduction of the new (the really new) work of art among them. The existing order is complete before the new work arrives; for order to persist after the supervention of novelty, the *whole* existing order must be, however slightly, altered; and so the relations, proportions, values of each work of art toward the whole are readjusted; and this is conformity between the old and the new."[1]

The notion of a simultaneous order is what holds the attention here, a sense of the past as present, and affected by the present, this quivering mass of "monuments" that undergo continuous revisionary assault. "No poet, no artist of any art, has his complete meaning alone," Eliot adds. This might come as a shock to young poets, who sometimes like to imagine they exist independent of what has gone before them. But no art of genuine interest can exist without an appreciable relationship with the past. A poet should not trouble over being influenced by, or responsive to, the poems that have already been written. Indeed, as Eliot notes, the most individual parts of a poet's work "may be those in which the dead poets, his ancestors, assert their immortality most vigorously." Lest anyone think that this influence affects only young poets or those in the earliest phase of their craft, Eliot says emphatically: "I do not mean the impressionable period of adolescence, but the period of full maturity."

Eliot's essay appeared in *The Sacred Wood* (1920), his immensely influential book of essays on poetry and criticism. Its haunting title alludes to the opening pages of Sir James Frazier's pioneering anthropological study *The Golden Bough*, first published in 1890, in which Frazier writes about the myth of a sacred wood ruled over by a powerful priest who continued to rule the forest until another priest came along and defeated him in battle. By deft allusion, Eliot was laying down the gauntlet, claiming priority in the sacred wood for himself, challenging those who would occupy this ground.

As with any poet who writes criticism, Eliot sought to create an environment in which his own work could prosper. This is natural enough. Eliot was a hugely innovative poet, but one whose work had deep and pervasive connections with everything that went before him. In some ways, *The Waste Land* might be read as another version of his essay on tradition and originality. It con-

sists of an elaborate mosaic of quotations from previous litera-
ture, all of them fragmentary, all filtered through the voice of the
poem. In the wake of the Great War, the "war to end all wars,"
Europe had become horribly shattered, physically and emotion-
ally. Traditional symbols appeared to have lost their power,
amounting to "a heap of broken images." Eliot surveyed this
ruined place, seeing "fear in a handful of dust." He ransacked the
universal library, looking for solace, for inspiration, often quite
desperately. "These fragments I have shored against my ruins,"
says a speaker at the end of *The Waste Land.*

Eliot was accused of plagiarism, of course. His work is an
anthology of his favorite lines and phrases, a tissue of allusions,
consisting of countless quotations from known and relatively
unknown works. The pseudo-scholarly footnotes tacked onto
the sequence provide a vague guide to his sources, but they are
comically inadequate and meant to be so. Eliot was rewriting the
past, not exhuming it. We see only the limbs of broken statues,
which lie scattered in the sands. In self-defense, Eliot once said
that bad poets imitate previous poets, while "good poets steal."
What he meant, I suspect, is that poetry should be considered a
form of rewriting. The intelligent and original artist, in any art,
confronts past works, revisits them eagerly, revises and remakes
them. New comes from old. Poetry is, indeed, plagiarism taken
to a sublime level, unafraid of imitation, taking energy from any
source that seems useful or relevant. The poet "steals" with a
sense of bravado—just as Shakespeare plundered everything of
interest to him from Raphael Holinshed's *Chronicles* to Thomas
North's translation of Plutarch to the literature of his contem-

poraries, from whose bush he plucked endless ripe berries. Or just as contemporary rappers take an earlier song and remix it, playing fast and loose with the original lyrics, extending the melodies, placing (or displacing) the lyrics and melody in a fresh context to extend or modify the meaning of the original song.

The nature, and purpose, of literary influence is a complex field in itself, and I shall only skim the surface here. But I hope to put forward some of the key ideas in the debate about "tradition" and "originality" and to suggest a fresh way of reading the past as something that both underlies the present and assists it, offering to poets a vast source of energy, a way of taking themselves that lifts them beyond rude self-assertion, even beyond the Romantic idea of poetry as self-expression. Poetry, in this reading of influence, becomes a communal act, one that retains some of the sublime self of the Romantic poet while it gestures toward what Adrienne Rich has called "the dream of a common language."

Poetry is also a form of education, for writers as well as readers. Poets quite naturally imitate their "precursors"—those who went before them in the art, and whom they "invent" for their own purposes (as Borges suggests), often misreading them in ways that allow their own craft to flourish in a vacuum they willfully create. It was the Greeks who put forward the influential idea that education was imitation of excellent examples. The ideal was perfection (*arete*), as King Peleus explains to his son Achilles in Homer's *Iliad*. The Greek method of education (*paideia*) involved emulation of this ideal. In literature, this meant that writers were asked to keep the goal of perfection before them. Given the Greek paranoia about imitation (*mimesis*)—the work of art is an imitation of nature, which is already an imperfect copy of something else—it should surprise no one that some anxiety of influence should have crept into the work of imitating excellence. A writer inevitably falls short of the ideal. A sense of belatedness, of having come to the task too late to make an original contribution to the art, seems inevitable.

There is a long history of belatedness connected with literary influence. The Romans, such as Catullus, Horace, and Virgil (to name a few major examples), lived in the shadow of Greek achievement, and each poet had to negotiate with a past that loomed heavily. They managed to negotiate this relationship brilliantly, as Gordon Williams shows in *Tradition and Originality in Roman Poetry.* He writes: "The simplest relationship which a Roman poet could establish with Greek poetry is that of translation." Poetry is always, in a sense, a translation of earlier poetry, as all art modifies and extends the art that precedes it. But the Romans went further, learning to treat Greek poetry "in the same way as they treated earlier Roman poetry: that is, a technique of literary allusion was developed which regarded Greek poetry as standing in the same relationship to the Roman poet as the earlier poetry of his own language."[2]

Poets writing in English have their own problems—Shakespeare, for one. Goethe, who is often regarded as the greatest of the German poets, thanked God that English was not his first language, so that he did not have to compete with Shakespeare directly. He warned against reading more than one play by Shakespeare per year, as the results could be overwhelming and discouraging.

In a long series of interviews with Johann Peter Eckermann, the elderly Goethe referred obsessively to Shakespeare. On January 2, 1824, Eckermann recorded the following: "We spoke about the greatness of Shakespeare, and what an unlucky position all English writers have, coming after that poetic giant. 'A dramatic talent,' Goethe continued, 'if it were significant, could not help taking notice of Shakespeare; indeed, it could not help studying him. But to study him is to become aware that Shakespeare has already exhausted the whole of human nature in all directions and in all depths and heights, and that for those who come after him, there remains nothing more to do. And where would an earnest soul, capable of appreciating genius, find the courage even to set pen to paper, if he were aware of such unfathomable and unreachable excellence already in existence? In that respect I was certainly better off in my dear Germany fifty years ago. I could very soon come to terms with the literature already in existence. It could not impose on me for long, and it could not much hold me back.'"[3]

Shakespeare himself may have experienced misgivings in his appropriations of work by others. Of course, he transformed whatever he adopted, absorbing influences easily and greedily. Yet at times he appears rattled in the face of rival poets, as in sonnet 86, where he refers to another poet, perhaps Christopher Marlowe or George Chapman, in grudging tones: "Was it his spirit, by spirits taught to write / Above a mortal pitch, that struck me dead?" One hears a distinct note of hesitation, too, in the epilogue to *Henry V,* where Shakespeare questions the power of his own imaginative enterprise: "Thus far, with rough and all-unable pen, / Our bending author hath pursued the story." In sonnet 76, he seems to wring his hands with self-doubt: "Why is my verse so barren of new pride, / So far from variation or quick change?" In fact, a sense of belatedness permeates several of his sonnets, including 18, 59, 106, and 130. In his plays, he adopted plots and scenes, even language, from earlier playwrights, and he acknowledges his debts openly in some cases, especially with regard to Ovid, as Jonathan Bate vividly demonstrates in *Shakespeare and Ovid* (1994).

For the most part, Shakespeare took what he pleased, often gleefully, as when he appropriates the balcony scene from Marlowe's *Jew of Malta* for his own *Romeo and Juliet,* hardly bothering to change the wording in places. With Ovid, he has fun with his precursor, for example in *As You Like It* (III, iii), where Touchstone and Audrey trade witticisms in the forest of Arden. Touchstone says: "I am here with thee and thy goats, as the most capricious poet, honest Ovid, was among the Goths." (Jaques overhears this, and makes a wistful aside: "O knowledge ill-inhabited, worse than Jove in a thatch'd house!") Such passages (and they are plentiful) reveal Shakespeare's endlessly protean dialogue with other poets, with little of the anxiety of influence that Harold Bloom identified.

With other major poets, the anxiety of their appropriations is more palpable. Ben Jonson, as Robert Watson has shown in *Literary Imperialism* (1999), was intensely conscious of his influences and precursors, doing battle in poem after poem. Milton was combative as well, and contended openly with Homer, Virgil, and Dante, each of whom he kept presently in mind as he wrote *Paradise Lost.* His epic is wildly contentious, attempting to reconcile pagan conventions (the conception of heroism, for example) with Christian ideals. It is hard to imagine that the epic struggle between God and Satan that Milton so fiercely renders in his poem does not, at least on an unconscious level, reflect his own battles with past authors. (Bloom meditates on this dynamic at length in *The Anxiety of Influence.*)

Milton was, after Shakespeare, the most complex and "monumental" British poet before the modern era, and he deeply affected those who came after him, including Wordsworth, Shelley, and Keats, each of whom wrote openly of their admiration. Critics have long pointed to stylistic and thematic affinities between Milton and later poets, as with *The Influence of Milton on English Poetry* (1922), a classic study by R. D. Havens. But there is something naively reductive about such studies, where echoes are traced in methodical fashion with little understanding of the psychological dynamics involved. In the mid-seventies, Bloom opened a way of thinking about influence that goes well beyond source hunting and the counting of allusions. For him influence necessarily involves "doing battle" with precursors and misreading them. Poems for Bloom exist only in their misreading by later poets. He refers to his approach as "antithetical criticism," which he describes as follows: "All criticisms that call themselves primary vacillate between tautology—in which the poem is and means itself—and reduction, a denial best delivered by the assertion that the meaning of a poem can only be a poem, but *another poem—a poem not itself.* And not a poem chosen with total arbitrariness, but any central poem by an indubitable precursor, even if the ephebe never read that poem. Source study is wholly irrelevant here; we are dealing with primal words, but antithetical meanings, and an ephebe's best misinterpretations may well be of poems he has never read."[4]

Eccentricity of style and personalized jargon aside, Bloom nevertheless gestures in directions that yield interesting results for critics. In essence, Bloom has swept up various Freudian notions and applied them to literary models, tracking the "development" of a poet in relation to his literary "fathers," whom he must cast off, even kill, to become "his own man." This is all very patriarchal, however intriguing and—in certain cases—appropriate. The young poet (the ephebe, as Bloom calls him—never really "her") determinably misreads his models, creating a space for himself in which originality can flourish. Often there is no specific poem from which a new poem arises; rather, the poet's aura (to use a term that Walter Benjamin, the great theorist of culture, liked) is what presides, against which the new poet struggles to superimpose a competing aura.

In most cases, I would argue, the influence of the precursor is subtle and almost invisible—even to the new poet. Poets find a source of energy in a prior body of work and attach themselves to it: not unlike attaching cables to a battery from one car to another, although the poet's work is hidden from public view. If the engine starts, the car is capable of running on its own. Thus, one can see a poet like Seamus Heaney connecting to the Anglo-

Saxon poets, to Gerard Manley Hopkins, to Dylan Thomas— and from those sources he got a manner of speaking, a bold alliterative sound, to which he has added his own yielding temper and whimsical angle of vision. From other poets, such as Robert Frost, he learned how to use the materials of rural life for poems. One can put a poem like Frost's "For Once, Then, Something" beside Heaney's "Personal Helicon" and see these poets working in a similar vein; in each case, the poet looks into a well, which is the well of memory, the well of the past. In each case, something is found at the bottom of the well or discovered in the act of looking. In Frost's poem, there is "something" at the bottom. "What was that whiteness?" the poet wonders. "Truth? A pebble of quartz?" This is quite a range, and highly unsettling. What Heaney discovers is himself in the process of looking or calling into the well: "I rhyme / To see myself, to set the darkness echoing." The "darkness" echoes in Heaney, with the self as sounding board, invisible and voiceless without the enabling convention of rhyme. Language makes the poet visible to himself.

My own sense is that, far from battling their precursors, poets more often consider themselves the benefactors of their literary forebears and engage in a kind of dialogue with them. This dialogue, in effect, is the stuff of culture.

Poetry is, indeed, a conversation, an ongoing and expansive "discussion" along certain lines. The whole point about literary conventions is that certain measures have already been established, and new poets have a place to begin. They accept or reject certain norms. They do their own versions of certain poems. They pay homage to their precursors, or reinvent them for their own purposes, distorting the ancestor (sometimes strenuously, as Bloom notes and tracks with vigor in his various books about literary influence). In my view, there is less intentional violence than Bloom and others in this vein see. It is simply poetic discourse, a mode of conversation, that unfolds.

Let us consider two famous examples of poets in dialogue. Here is Wordsworth's "London, 1802," a sonnet of considerable force:

> MILTON! thou shouldst be living at this hour:
>   England hath need of thee: she is a fen
>   Of stagnant waters: altar, sword, and pen,
> Fireside, the heroic wealth of hall and bower,
> Have forfeited their ancient English dower
>   Of inward happiness. We are selfish men;
>   O raise us up, return to us again,
> And give us manners, virtue, freedom, power!
> Thy soul was like a Star, and dwelt apart;
>   Thou hadst a voice whose sound was like the sea:
>   Pure as the naked heavens, majestic, free,
>   So didst thou travel on life's common way,
> In cheerful godliness; and yet thy heart
>   The lowliest duties on herself did lay.

Wordsworth proceeds on several levels, praising his hero while making sure to disparage contemporary England. The poem refers not to Milton but to the country and the poet's time. This "fen / Of stagnant waters" has obviously worn the young Wordsworth down. He looks back fondly to a time when England was a republic under Oliver Cromwell, not a suffocating monarchy (as he saw it, at least in his youth). He regrets the squandering of this inheritance ("dower") of "inward happiness." The accusation becomes strong: "We are selfish men." And so he turns to Milton as though to God: "O raise us up." One almost believes the poet is writing a psalm here. Milton is elevated above the rest, becoming "like a Star." He "dwelt apart" from the mess below, "Pure as the naked heavens, majestic, free." But Milton (in Wordsworth's regard) also managed to keep in touch with ordinary life, the "common way." He worked in the vineyards, doing political work for the Cromwell regime, and so forth.

Note what Shelley does with this poem, and its dynamics, in his own poem dedicated to *his* precursor, Wordsworth:

> Poet of Nature, thou hast wept to know
> That things depart which never may return:
> Childhood and youth, friendship and love's first glow,
> Have fled like sweet dreams, leaving thee to mourn.
> These common woes I feel. One loss is mine,
> Which thou too feel'st, yet I alone deplore.
> Thou wert as a lone star, whose light did shine
> On some frail bark in winter's midnight roar:
> Thou hast like to a rock-built refuge stood
> Above the blind and battling multitude:
> In honoured poverty thy voice did weave
> Songs consecrate to truth and liberty,—
> Deserting these, thou leavest me to grieve,
> Thus having been, that thou shouldst cease to be.
>   ["To Wordsworth"]

This poem could hardly exist without the Wordsworth example before it. It assumes a knowledge of the earlier poem and continues the discussion. Shelley begins as well with an address or apostrophe to the precursor, his "Poet of Nature." It recognizes a missing element in the world: the loss of a great figure. It adds to this Wordsworth's own obsessive consideration of the losses everywhere in abundance. Yet the consolidation of all losses into "one loss" is striking, even shocking. Wordsworth laments the passing of so much glory in his work overall, whereas Shelley gathers this sentiment into his loss of Wordsworth's power as a *political* poet, one dedicated to "truth and liberty"—a strange move here, as Wordsworth was still very much alive when Shelley wrote this poem.

Shelley pulls no punches. He celebrates the power of Wordsworth in his prime as a "lone star" akin to the Milton whom Wordsworth had praised in exactly the same terms, a poet "above the blind and battling multitude." But there is a chilling dismissal here as well, given the fact that Wordsworth was alive and (as a poet, in Shelley's view) unwell. Working from the example of Wordsworth, Shelley employed the high and low vectors to suggest that Wordsworth (like Milton) managed to work in "honoured poverty," the realm of "life's common way." But the fact that this is no longer happening is felt as a strong backdraft.

There is doubtless an anxiety of influence in Shelley's poem. One can feel the aggression in his attempt to put the great master, this Poet of Nature, in his place; he implicitly repositions Wordsworth in relation to Milton and downgrades him. There is a note of falseness in the "lone star" move in Shelley's poem. The mirroring of Wordsworth's structure also has the effect of denigrating Wordsworth, for the terms of comparison are not equal here. Shelley cannot say "thou shouldst be living at this hour" because Wordsworth was indeed living. But one hears that phrase sound beneath the opening line in the poem anyway, an ironic if somewhat covert echo of "England, 1802."

More commonly, poets engage in less combative dialogue or "conversation" with their precursors. There is not so much an Oedipal struggle between father and son as a bold assumption of parity—the "new" poet merely assumes equality with the "older" one, defying history and time. The new poet slips into the stream of conversation. To change the metaphor, the young poet takes his or her place at the high table of art, agreeing or disagreeing with the elders, offering fresh lines of argument, countering image with image, phrase with phrase. The contest is lively, but it is productive, at least when it works well.

Often the dialogue between poets is intimate and, to a degree, unseen by most readers. Let me conclude with a train of three poems. In the sixteenth century, the following lyric appeared anonymously:

Western wind, when wilt thou blow,
The small rain down can rain?
Christ if my love were in my arms,
And I in my bed again.

This is a classic poem of love and loss, a poem in which the poet expresses despair because of the lover's absence. The formality of the first lines (with their incomparable lyric beauty) stands in contrast to the last two lines, where the colloquial use of "Christ" as a swear word and the intimate nature of the expression take away the reader's breath with its candor. The wind represents time and distance, and the question is given a peculiar urgency by that ravishing second line, with its evenly spread beats, which makes the implicit iambs (the abstract rhythmic potential of the line) so effective. A similar effect occurs in the third line: the abstract line is iambic tetrameter, but the poet reverses the initial foot brilliantly, putting the weight on the initial word, then creating an anapest of sorts with "if my love." This was done, of course, only semi-consciously; poets don't sit down and say to themselves: "Hey, I'll just reverse that iamb." They have been trained in the use of metrical verse, and they understand what sorts of effects can be achieved in various ways.

Robert Penn Warren had the poem deeply in mind when he wrote "Blow, West Wind":

I know, I know—though the evidence
Is lost, and the last who might speak are dead.
Blow, west wind, blow, and the evidence, O

Is lost, and wind shakes the cedar, and O,
I know how the kestrel hung over Wyoming,
Breast reddened in sunset, and O, the cedar

Shakes, and I know how cold
Was the sweat on my father's mouth, dead.
Blow, west wind, blow, shake the cedar, I know

How once I, as boy, crouching at creekside,
Watched, in the sunlight, a handful of water
Drip, drip, from my hand. The drops—they were bright!

But you believe nothing, with the evidence lost.

Warren has picked up a line of feeling and a movement as well. He seems to have taken up where "Western wind" has left off, and we begin the poem in medias res: in the middle of a thought, as it were. The poem adds local color: the kestrel in Wyoming. He includes small autobiographical touches in ways that make the poem his own, for example when the poet emerges as a boy "crouching at creekside." To the wind that sweeps through the earlier poem Warren has added water. There is no absent lover in Warren's poem, only the absent father; but one feels the presence of an absent lover anyway, a leftover feeling from the earlier poem from which it (however obliquely) arose. One also hears in the background other poetic language, such as Shakespeare's *King Lear,* Act III, scene ii: "Blow, wind, and crack your cheeks!" (The effect of this massive echo is incalculable, but it certainly amplifies the emotional impact of the poem.) I would guess that Warren had other sources for this poem, too, for he had drenched himself in poetry. My point is merely that, far from contending in some Oedipal way with his anonymous precursor, he merely assumes the right to sit at the same table and add his own voice, which is underwritten by the earlier voice, in the model of the palimpsest.

I have myself added something to this line of conversation, in "I Was There":

I say it, I was there.
No matter what the yellow wind has taken,
I was there, with you.
We have walked out early in the spring
beside the river, when the sun's red shield

was caught in branches
and the bud-tips bled.
We have plucked ripe berries from a hill of brush
in mid-July,
and watched the days go down in flames
in late September,
when the poplar shook its foil.
We have walked on snow in January light:
the long white fields were adamantly bright.
I say it, I was there.
No matter that the evidence is gone,
we heard the honking of the long black geese
and saw them float beyond the town.
Gone all those birds, loose-wristed leaves,
the snowfire, days
we cupped like water in our hands.
So much has slipped through fragile hands.
The evidence is lost, but not these words.
I say it, I was there.

I add a poem of my own to this chain only because I can talk personally about how I worked with earlier voices, not merely guessing about sources and influences (although a poet is often less aware of sources than his or her critics, as poets can work semiconsciously, even—at times—unconsciously). When I wrote this, I had in mind both "Western wind" and, even more vividly, the Warren poem, with its urgency, and the sense that "the evidence, O / is lost, and wind shakes the cedar." It was the tone that stuck with me in both poems, the sense of a poet trying desperately to recover a feeling, to preserve a sense of enhanced life in love. I never felt myself in competition with either the anonymous author of "Western wind" or Warren. Warren was a close friend and mentor of mine, someone to whom I brought my early poems for advice and confirmation. I was certainly influenced by him: for decades I read his poems closely and often imitated them. I did so unabashedly, as poetry almost always involves imitation at some level. Even when a poet is mature, as Eliot notes, he allows himself to respond to earlier work, and lets the earlier work shine through his own.

Poetry is conversation, and poets enter into the discussion wherever they are, as they will. They sometimes contend boldly, even aggressively, with earlier poets, misreading them willfully. Often they merely accept the precursor as a beloved inspiration and continue to work a vein opened by that poet. There is, on the whole, a sense of lively dialogue in poetry, which rarely exists independent of earlier work, as poetry depends for its effects on conventions. The tradition is a living organism, and poets come to it keenly, eager to remember things they have read and heard, eager to modify and extend what has gone before them. It is within this work of recollection and extension that true originality lives and prospers.

6 form and freedom

Oh! Blessed rage for order, pale
  Ramon,
The maker's rage to order words of
  the sea,
Words of the fragrant portals,
  dimly-starred,
And of ourselves and of our
  origins,
In ghostlier demarcations, keener
  sounds.

WALLACE STEVENS

I think I put whatever orderliness
I've got into my poems, and the
rest is chaos.

MARY JO SALTER

The formal patterns of poetry help us to order our thoughts, to make sense of our lives. Poetry emerges from this primordial "rage for order," the passion that Stevens refers to. It is a *blessed* rage for order, he suggests, because it helps us to live our lives by allowing us to find "ghostlier demarcations," which are lines or boundaries between mind and world, between self and nature, matter and spirit. In finding these words, the poet reconnects us to some prior reality, linking us back (as in *re-ligio:* the root of *religion*) to our origins; that is, in poetry, we encounter a language that is more concrete, more visual, more sensual, than the language of abstract thought. In its attraction to form, the language of poetry (those "keener sounds" Stevens refers to) finds patterns that correspond in some way to what, for lack of a better word, one might refer to as "truth," although the term itself is distracting (if not misleading).

The truth of poetry is symbolic truth, in that it cannot be verified by conventional means. It differs massively from scientific or philosophical truth, both of which make truth claims that lie outside the boundaries of poetry. One reads a poem and "knows" whether it makes sense or doesn't. The truth of poetry inheres in the language itself, the web or "text" (from *texere,* "to weave"). But the poem is also a labyrinth. One makes a journey through the poem, from beginning to end, moving within the space of the work, its boundaries, tracking its labyrinth or pattern. As Gabriel Josipovici writes in *The World and the Book,* it is only so long as the poem is being read, "so long, that is, as the human imagination is traveling along the arteries of the labyrinth, that we are aware of the boundaries, and therefore of what lies beyond them."[1]

Poetry is liturgical, however secular. That is, it aligns itself with ceremonial traditions, where men and women gather (often in a sacred space, such as a chapel or sacred grove or ring of standing stones) to chant their praises to God and reaffirm their connection to the community as well as to confirm (even explore) their own identities. In this sense, poetry provides the consolations of religion, "the satisfactions of belief," as Stevens put it. These satisfactions are deep and reassuring; in fact, without them, the world would seem oddly shapeless and disembodied, inarticulate, lacking a ground. The community would remain invisible to itself, and individuals would not see the boundaries of self as well as the boundaries of the body politic.

Emily Dickinson understood the use of form as consolation. In one of her poems, she writes: "After great pain, a formal feeling comes." Anyone can understand this feeling, which is a need as well. When a loved one dies, for example, a funeral or memorial service follows: a formal event that mirrors the urge toward form that comes in the wake of tragedy. The ceremony is useful in helping those in grief to assuage their feelings, to organize their thoughts and recollections, to imagine themselves in relation to the loss that has caused the pain. There is something about the ceremony itself that assists in making the pain endurable by, in obvious ways, naming it. Without the ceremony, those in grief would experience a mess of unnamed, even unrecognized, feelings. What Dickinson calls "the letting go" in this poem can happen only in the context of form.

She herself operated on the assumption that form could liberate. For the most part, she wrote in the extremely ordinary form called common measure, the pattern that she found in many Protestant hymns, such as "Amazing Grace." Her poems, with their wild energies, became possible within the boundaries of simple rhyme and rhythm, which have a strangely ceremonious feel to them, as if written for a private chapel service. Like many in the tradition of Romanticism, she saw the poet's job as discerning "divinest Sense" that to the world at large looks like madness. Let's consider a short poem to see how she operates within the affirming limits of poetry to find a kind of eerie freedom:

Much Madness is divinest Sense—
To a discerning Eye—
Much Sense—the starkest Madness—
'Tis the Majority
In this, as All, prevail—
Assent—and you are sane—
Demur—you're straightway dangerous—
And handled with a Chain—

The poem adheres broadly to the usual form of common measure, alternating a four-beat line with a three-beat line, rhyming on every other line, a form that also recalls the ballad stanza, and so chimes with communal forms. Yet Dickinson exhibits her own madness, wrestling with the form itself and its conventions. First, there are those dashes: Dickinson casts off the usual conventions of punctuation, eschewing periods and commas, semicolons, colons, question marks. She brings in those bold capitals, as if she were writing in German. She enjambs her lines fiercely, allowing the sense of the line to spill over the breaks, as when she says that "'Tis the Majority / In this, as All, prevail—." She uses slant rhyme: "majority" chimes with "Eye." Most important, she roughs up the iambic pattern, as in the third line, where "Much" and "Sense" have equal weight, and each constitutes a foot of verse. The same happens again in the fifth line, with equal stress landing on "In" and "this." The airy freedom of the poem derives, therefore, from the ways in which Dickinson plays with the form; the breaking of form enacts the very independence trumpeted in the poem. The poet's "discerning Eye" sees beyond the labyrinth of the formal boundaries, glimpsing the dark on either side of the light.

As noted in Chapter 1, it was often suggested by historians of literature (especially in the eighteenth and nineteenth centuries) that poetry had its origins in the chants of primitive people. One can only guess at such things, of course. Poetry actually comes into view in the Western world during the eighth century B.C., when the Greeks learned alphabet writing from the Phoenicians. One assumes that before the invention of writing, there was still song and story and liturgy. The Homeric epics, the *Iliad* and *Odyssey*, were possibly sung aloud in a kind of chant. Song itself has deep roots in peasant (agricultural) society: Homer himself refers to the traditions of singing when the harvest was brought in, singing laments for the dead at funerals, and singing songs to appease Apollo in times of danger. We are told that Circe sings as she weaves. And so forth: Homer's was a singing or chanting culture, and the lyre formed a part of this.

Lyric verse—in a literal sense—is poetry sung to the accompaniment of a lyre. (It is possible that the Homeric poems were "sung" with lyres strummed or pipes played.) One can see from the poetry of early Greece that there was a choral element to this verse, which presupposes a dramatic or liturgical setting. There were religious and harvest festivals in abundance, and funeral ceremonies, and all manner of public gatherings where chanting formed part of the experience. By the fifth century B.C., dramatic performances had become a central aspect of Athenian life, with celebrations of Dionysus occurring in the spring and taking the form of verse plays, which featured a choral element and resembled liturgical occasions. In all these public rituals, the community gathered and saw itself and could articulate its deepest longings, its highest aspirations. Not surprisingly, this poetry was highly conventional, which is to say that the lines adhered to strict meters and stanza patterns.

Greek verse was measured, consisting of feet determined by patterns of vowels and the number of feet per line. In Latin poetry, too, verse was measured. Poets counted the number of feet per line, and each foot consisted of a set pattern of long and short vowels. One could easily measure the "quantity" of the vowels as long or short. These were strictly set and readily apparent to the listener. This form of counting out the feet depended almost wholly on the quantity of the vowels. There was a rhythmic element here, too, in both Latin and Greek, but rhythms were less defined or determined than the pattern of the vowels. The transposition of quantitative meter to English verse was never simple, however, and has led to some confusion.

English poetry is stressed poetry, in the tradition of Old German and Anglo-Saxon verse. Poets pay little or no attention to the quantity of vowels, listening instead for the number of stresses (hard beats) per line. And so a line of pentameter will have five beats per line, with one foot equal to one stressed syllable and any number of unstressed syllables. In the nineteenth century, Gerard Manley Hopkins (a poet and classical scholar) called this sprung rhythm. But Hopkins didn't invent this form. Most poetry in English is "sprung," in that poets focus on the number of stresses, allowing the number of unstressed or partially stressed syllables to vary.

To see how rhythm and meter work to produce the effects that we call "poetic," consider "On My First Son," by Ben Jonson:

Farewell, thou child of my right hand, and joy;
My sin was too much hope of thee, loved boy.
Seven years thou wert lent to me, and I thee pay,
Exacted by thy fate, on the just day.
Oh, could I lose all father now! For why
Will man lament the state he should envy?
To have so soon 'scaped world's and flesh's rage,
And, if no other misery, yet age?
Rest in soft peace, and, asked, say here doth lie
Ben Jonson, his best piece of poetry.

For whose sake, henceforth, all his vows be such
As what he loves may never like too much.

This is an elegy on the death of Jonson's seven-year-old son Benjamin (the name in Hebrew means "child of my right hand," hence the allusion in the first line). Let's consider the metrical and rhythmical aspects of this poignant, affecting poem. It is written in couplets of iambic pentameter, one of the most common forms of poetry, especially during the early seventeenth century (the form was perfected by Alexander Pope in the next century). Jonson realizes that a singsong effect would come from adhering too closely to the iambic foot, in which an unstressed syllable is followed by a stressed one. And so he begins: "Farewell." The stress divides evenly here in spoken English. Only in the "theoretical" (or hypothetical) version of the line would it read with the accent on "well." "Thou child" seems to have even stresses on "thou" and "child," and "right hand" seems evenly stressed as well. In the next line, "loved boy" is equally stressed. The resulting sound seems highly pressured, as if the poet were barely able to contain his grief; there is indeed "a formal feeling" in these lines, which points to "great pain," as in Dickinson's line.

In formal verse, the effects of poetry (strong emotion, memorable phrasing, musical beauty) arise from the contrast between the theoretical possibility of the line (*te-tum, te-tum, te-tum, te-tum, te-tum*) and its actual spoken quality. The theoretical line organizes the spoken line, gives it shape and body, producing an effect not unlike memory. But the memory here is the memory of other lines of perfect blank verse, or an intuition of the perfect, abstract version of the line in question. If you spoke the first two lines of Jonson's poem in their abstract potential, you would hideously distort the vernacular sound. When we get down to the concluding phase of the poem, which begins with the address to the boy, "Rest in soft peace," there is a singular strength in that line that derives from the confounding of metrical expectation. One hears (faintly) the abstract iambic feet, with the emphasis on "in" and "peace." But one overrides this abstract possibility, pushes over it, as the emotion overwhelms the vessel of the verse itself. It is as if truth suddenly were speaking, ignoring all boundaries, even the boundary of death. The verse form itself creates the possibility for immense freedom and release from form. These would remain impossible without the self-imposed restraints of formal poetry.

Thomas Campion, in the seventeenth century, defined poetry as a system of linked sounds. This is a useful definition, especially when thinking about form. During the Anglo-Saxon period, the formal elements that held poetry together were alliteration and stress. Rhyme and meter were much less relevant, and end rhymes rare because in Anglo-Saxon there were few rhyming words. The opposite is true of the Italian language, where rhymes are abundant (even the phone book rhymes in Italy). And so elaborate rhymes and stanza patterns evolved: the word *stanza,* in fact, is an Italian word meaning "room," as in the rooms of a building.

When the Norman French invaded England in 1066, they brought with them the vast vocabulary of Latin, with its various dialects (Italian, French, Spanish, Portuguese). Now rhyming on vowels became possible as a way of linking the various sounds of a poem, and this rhyming boasted not only end rhymes but internal rhymes as well, or assonance. (Note that alliteration, so important for the Anglo-Saxon poets, might well be thought of as rhyming on consonants.) Any handbook of poetry will reveal the huge variety of stanza possibilities, ranging from simple ballad stanzas to such things as ottava rima, an intricate eight-line stanza whose first six lines rhyme alternately, while the last two lines form a rhyming couplet. Various larger forms were imported from Italy, including the sonnet and the villanelle.

Most of the poetry written in English from the time of Chaucer through the nineteenth century was formal: the linking devices were fairly conventional. Meter powered much of the unrhymed verse from Shakespeare through Milton and Wordsworth to the magnificent blank verse of Wallace Stevens or Robert Frost. Rhyme also played a role, as did stanza patterns, in the poetry of these centuries. By the twentieth century, however, free verse had become the norm, though formal verse continued to flourish as well—and persists in contemporary poetry, where it has enjoyed a revival in recent years. Most poets of note have used both formal verse and free verse as needed, depending on the subject or desired effects, although Frost rejected free verse as being "too much like playing tennis without the net." But ever since Whitman, the possibilities (and flexibility) of free verse have proven so attractive that poets can hardly resist using it.

The term is misleading, however. There is no such thing as free verse. That is, the verse called "free" might better be described as poetry with variable meters and, in most cases, internal rhyming. (Even here, there is often end rhyming, although the pattern will be irregular.) Frequently, poets writing free verse employ stanzas, which serve to gather chunks of material, often as a "step" in the narrative of a poem. But free verse, if well done, is no easier to write than formal poetry; in many ways, it's harder. Form itself is a vessel that, with a modicum of skill, any poet can fill. The demands of free verse are such that only a poet with an unusually good ear as well as an innate sense of form can work successfully in the genre.

Whitman, of course, "invented" free verse, although he had models of a kind in the King James Bible and Blake. But the modern free verse poem has its origins in *Song of Myself* and in such nuggets as "A Noiseless Patient Spider"—

> A noiseless patient spider,
> I mark'd where on a little promontory it stood isolated,
> Mark'd how to explore the vacant vast surrounding,
> It launch'd forth filament, filament, filament, out of itself,
> Ever unreeling them, ever tirelessly speeding them.
>
> And you O my soul where you stand,
> Surrounded, detached, in measureless oceans of space,
> Ceaselessly musing, venturing, throwing, seeking the spheres to
>   connect them,
> Till the bridge you will need be form'd, till the ductile anchor hold,
> Till the gossamer thread you fling catch somewhere, O my soul.

Each line, like a leaf, expands fully, finding its exact and seemingly preordained organic shape. The first line sets the image in place and leaves it hanging in poetic and syntactical space, the object of a sentence whose subject, "I," doesn't arrive until the next line. Note the parallelism that Whitman uses to organize lines 2 and 3 with the repetition of the verb "mark'd." The poet "marks" or notes the spider. The repeated word "filament" provides a driving rhythm in the fourth line. Rhyme occurs but in a subtle way, with "surrounding" at the end of the third line chiming with "unreeling" and "speeding"—these words finding further echoes in the second stanza with "musing, venturing, throwing, seeking." There is an alliterative aspect as well: "vacant vast" is marvelous. A remarkable management of vowels and consonants brightens the fifth line, which concludes the first of the poem's two five-line stanzas: "Ever unreeling them, ever tirelessly speeding them." Again, there is parallelism in the syntax. In the second stanza, where Whitman turns the spider into a symbol, we begin and end with the address to the poet's soul. The poem concludes with more parallel phrasing: "Till the bridge," "till the ductile anchor," and "Till the gossamer thread" all connect to "catch" in the final line. There are no abrupt or ill-considered line breaks. The words appear to unfold from within, to "catch" on some original and invisible form discovered in the act of writing. This is masterly, and deeply considered, writing. In no rational use of the term could this be called "free" verse, for Whitman has bought perfection dearly, having brought a wide range of skills and imaginative force to bear in a short space.

The Imagists, writing in the early twentieth century, also brought a mastery to free verse form that demands our attention. Amy Lowell, a leading proponent of this movement, had astonishing control of her verse, however free it seemed, as we see in "The Taxi"—

> When I go away from you
> The world beats dead
> Like a slackened drum.
> I call out for you against the jutted stars
> And shout into the ridges of the wind.
> Streets coming fast,
> One after the other,
> Wedge you away from me,
> And the lamps of the city prick my eyes
> So that I can no longer see your face.
> Why should I leave you,
> To wound myself upon the sharp edges of the night?

This is another "system of linked sounds." Lowell uses a good deal of subtle alliteration: "dead" meets "drum" with a thud. Those "w" sounds carry forward from "When" and "away" through "world" and "wind." She picks up the "w" sounds again in the last five lines, with "Wedge" connecting to "away" and "Why" and "wound." The repetition of "you" becomes a baseline note from first to last. Lowell has a fine ear, so that each line plays neatly off the previous line, and there is a restrained formality about the poem. The imagery is sharp, the language consistently concrete and figurative in clever ways, such as her notion of the world beating "dead / Like a slackened drum."

A more casual use of free verse can be found in William Carlos Williams, another poet who belonged (to some extent) to the Imagist school, and whose verse often seems offhand and underwritten. Nevertheless, it stays in the mind, as in, for example, "To a Poor Old Woman"—

> munching a plum on
> the street a paper bag
> of them in her hand
>
> They taste good to her
> They taste good
> To her. They taste
> Good to her
>
> You can see it by
> the way she gives herself
> to the one half
> sucked out in her hand
>
> Comforted
> a solace of ripe plums
> seeming to fill the air
> They taste good to her

The erratic use of capital letters at the beginning of some lines is calculated, giving the poem a heightened aura of casualness, as if the poet were merely taking notes, not shaping a poem. But he *is* shaping it. The lines are short, more or less of equal length, yet each catches the eye and fills the ear. The line breaks seem casual, perhaps too fiercely enjambed, as if the poet merely chopped up prose into poetic bits. This seems especially true of the third stanza. Yet Williams does use the form carefully: the second stanza breaks up the repeated line in irregular ways, with repeated words ("taste" and "good") echoing loudly, three times each in a short stanza! Indeed, the last line of the poem gathers up the previously scattered phrases, in summary form: "They taste good to her." The last stanza grows from a witty construction in the second line: a "solace of ripe plums." This "solace" seems "to fill the air." The consoling image pleases all the senses, especially sound (in the beauty of the line) but also taste, for we know what ripe plums taste like. Williams knows exactly what he is doing and does it well; the poem is "free" only in that the lines are slightly irregular in length, and the rhymes subtle and internal; "munching" marries well with "plum on" just as "Comforted" vaguely chimes with "plums."

Free verse requires of the poet an acute attention to the shape of the line, which has to be broken for effect, not just cut off. If there is enjambment this must be done consciously, for a reason. Writers of free verse use a whole range of poetic effects, including rhyme (irregular end rhymes and assonance) and meter (variable), although in the best examples rhyme will occur as a kind of echo effect, while meter provides a pulse. Countless poetical techniques, including alliteration and parallelism, can be used to link sounds in a poem. For the most part, skilled poets master these techniques to such a degree that the effects associated with poetry occur naturally. The poets may be hardly aware of them as they write, but that has no bearing on their power to organize the language and to make it memorable.

There is no such thing as formless poetry, as all poetry is by definition form. The poet is a maker (*poetry* itself is derived from *poiein,* the Greek word meaning "to make"), shaping words, creating a pattern of experience on the page. Whether writing in a traditional form such as the sonnet or free verse, the poet employs a range of conventions, and these provide limits or boundaries— a grid of sorts, through which the light of reality may shine. The poem is an artifact, a made thing, standing apart from reality; but reality inheres in the particulars. More intriguingly, the wider possibilities of human consciousness become visible at the edges of the form itself. In this way, poetry becomes useful, helping readers to comprehend their lives, to catch their ideas in language, to see through this language to what lies beyond it.

7 the politics of poetry

You must write, and read, as if your life depended on it.

ADRIENNE RICH

My silences have not protected me. Your silence will not protect you.

AUDRE LORDE

Poetry, let us say, whether it belongs to an old political dispensation or aspires to express a new one, has to be a working model of inclusiveness.

SEAMUS HEANEY

oetry matters, in part, because of its potential for political expression. While a good deal of poetry has nothing whatever to do with politics, or touches on issues that might be called "political" only in a tangential way, poets who willfully choose to ignore all political dimensions risk pushing their work into the margins. It is important for poets to read the world around them and to respond to that world in their own fashion: not in slogans that can be printed on posters or slapped onto bumpers but in urgent, astute ways that reflect the injustice and immorality everywhere in evidence, even sad abundance. At their best, poets suggest useful ways to think and feel about these things, and picture them clearly. Poets do not offer solutions, however. They offer a depth of understanding, and a language adequate to the visions they summon.

All times are violent and crass, with idiocy in high places and a lack of moral standards in the political sphere; but since the attacks of September 11, 2001, in New York City and Washington, there has been a renewed urgency among poets, who have found a receptive audience for words that seem true, that capture complex emotions in a language adequate to the time. One could hardly turn on the radio in the weeks following September 11 without hearing poems read aloud. (One poem that was frequently chosen was W. H. Auden's haunting "September 1, 1939," which refers to the day the Germans overran Poland.) In a real sense, poetry provides a moral standard for expression, one against which political rhetoric must be judged—and is often found wanting.

A common assumption is that poetry reflects the voice of a nation. This is nonsense, as poets rarely speak for anyone but themselves. They may represent a certain group—Chicanos or gays, for example—but if they do so, they do this in a unique manner, finding a way to express the needs or experience of the group in their own measure and style. In fact, there is something antithetical to the project of poetry to imagine a blended or unified voice of any kind; even the notion of a representative voice—Whitman's inclusive democratic persona—requires some analysis and elaboration. No two original poets sound alike, and there has rarely been much solidarity among poets.

As far as political sympathies go, it has long been observed that most of the major poets of the early twentieth century—Yeats, Frost, Eliot, Stevens, and Ezra Pound—would fall into the category of "conservative" or "reactionary" rather than "liberal" or "progressive." Yeats, for example, identified rather aggressively at times with the upper crust; he consistently disdained the middle classes, those merchants who "fumble in a greasy till" in their shops, counting their pennies. His zeal for Irish independence was hardly a sign of his radical political sensibility; it was driven by old-fashioned patriotism, a love of his own land, its history and legends. It was also motivated by his affection for a woman, Maud Gonne, who encouraged his nationalist stance.

Frost was a natural conservative, like most farmers, but a cranky and unpredictable one. He encouraged his students at Amherst College to abandon their studies and join the army during World War I, upsetting his colleagues, many of whom were against the war. During the Great Depression, Frost derided Franklin Roosevelt and the New Deal, which he considered immoral because it discouraged people from seeking work and allowed the government to make decisions about the lives of people who (in his view) could make these decisions for themselves. His poems "New Hampshire" and "Provide, Provide" represent an expression of these attitudes, and they remain excellent examples of political poetry that comes from a conservative angle.

Indeed, when Frost read "Provide, Provide" to audiences in the fifties, he often emphasized the point about people making their own decisions by hammering home the last three lines:

> Better to go down dignified
> With boughten friendship at your side
> Than none at all. Provide, provide!

In other words, you must provide for yourself by whatever means you can muster. "Make the whole stock exchange your own!" if you must, to ensure that you will be taken care of in your old age. "Boughten friendship"—nurses and assistants who look after you—are less good than friends and relatives; but their help beats loneliness and poverty and despair. At readings, Frost would pause at the end of this poem, having emphasized the last two words, then say in a sly, droll tone: "Provide for yourself. Or somebody else is going to provide for you—and you aren't going to like that, are you?"

The intersection of morality and politics in Frost can be observed in "Two Tramps in Mud Time," a poem about work and the right to work. The speaker in the poem is cutting wood on his farm in the country, "giving a loose to my soul," he says. He enjoys the labor thoroughly, regarding it as both his "vocation" and his "avocation." The work must be done, and he likes doing it himself. But two "tramps" appear suddenly "Out of the mud." Apparently these "tramps" know how to cut wood: Frost refers to them as "Men of the woods and lumberjacks" who "judged me by their appropriate tool," the ax. This poem appeared during a period of great economic stress in the United States, when men of good character but no luck roamed the country looking for odd jobs. They hoped to pick up a little work in order to pay for a meal and, perhaps, regain a little of their lost self-respect. The first of the tramps walks away from the speaker, seeing that he obviously takes great pleasure in cutting the wood, but the second lingers. "He wanted to take my job for pay," Frost says. There is an unmistakable note of resentment there.

The crucial juncture in the poem occurs in the penultimate stanza:

Nothing on either side was said.
They knew they had but to stay their stay
And all their logic would fill my head:
As that I had no right to play

With what was another man's work for gain.
My right might be love but theirs was need.
And where the two exist in twain
Theirs was the better right—agreed.

The poet agrees with this line of reasoning, though with reluctance, as he takes pleasure in the work of splitting wood and hates to relinquish his hobby to another man just because that man happens to need the work. Frost's poem takes a complex moral stand as the speaker in the poem admits that "need" takes precedence over what he calls "love." Yet Frost is stacking the deck here by choosing "love" for the counterbalancing term to "need." The way has been prepared for the final stanza:

But yield who will to their separation,
My object in living is to unite
My avocation and my vocation
As my two eyes make one in sight.
Only where love and need are one,
And the work is play for mortal stakes,
Is the deed ever really done
For Heaven and the future's sakes.

One always wishes for a situation in life where "need" runs in the same direction as love. But the context of the poem disallows an easy reading of this stanza; Frost demands of the reader a willingness to occupy a position in which one may have to sacrifice "love" for "need." Need wins in the end, as it must, even though it is not—at least for the speaker in the poem (and probably the reader as well)—a comfortable choice. But moral choices are rarely comfortable—a point that seems central to the project of this poem. It might be argued that the discomfort itself is the point of the poem, which plays out the drama of moral choice in considerable detail, disallowing easy judgments.

A number of poets (myself among them) were invited to a symposium at the White House on "Poetry and the American Voice" in 2003—not long before the ill-fated invasion of Iraq. Three of the American poets to be discussed were Walt Whitman, Emily Dickinson, and Langston Hughes. The First Lady, Laura Bush, apparently hoped to keep politics out of the discussion; when it became obvious that this would not happen, she canceled the symposium, expressing disappointment that poets felt the need to bring in politics. Her dream of a politics-free poetry was illusory, of course. It would have been difficult to keep politics out of the conversation, as the political dimension of poetry is central to its overall project. This seems especially true of Whitman and Hughes, who took themselves as rebels. But even Dickinson had a fierce moral edge that some would call political.

Whitman represents a fairly quarrelsome voice in poetry: "I hear it was charged against me that I sought to destroy institutions," he intoned in a fierce poem, "Calamus"; "But really I am neither for nor against institutions." He supported only one institution: "The institution of the dear love of comrades." In poem after poem, Whitman speaks out against the immorality of slavery and poverty. He exhibits no interest in pretty poems that simply set out to entertain readers: "The words of true poems do not merely please." He was a democrat with a small "d," a man who considered himself a representative of the people. Yet there is a very special (and uniquely American) idea of democracy and its relationship to the individual in the opening salvo of *Song of Myself*—

> I celebrate myself, and sing myself.
> And what I assume you shall assume,
> For every atom belonging to me as good belongs to you.

A radical sense of democracy underlies such a position, with its communal view of body and soul. Whitman will allow no boundaries between "me" and "you," between "mine" and "yours." In singing himself, he sings everyone else. There was never a voice quite like his, and few have followed in exactly his mold— although Whitman has been hugely influential. "I am the mate and companion of people," he writes, celebrating them all in this magnificent poem: rank and file, highborn and lowborn, young and old, black and white. He is "Walt Whitman, a kosmos" but "no stander above men and women or apart from them." The revolutionary note sounds in every line, often in images that recommend self-transformation. "Unscrew the locks from the doors!" he implores us. "Unscrew the doors themselves from their jambs!"

This is political only by implication, but a fair number of Whitman's poems are overtly so, dealing with issues of the day, as Jerome Loving notes, suggesting that Whitman "introduced politics into poetry in *Leaves of Grass* by invoking the concerns of middle America, its occupations and need for jobs, its confusion about slavery—its need for spiritual leaders other than conventional religionists, its democracy and hatred of kings and aristocracies as well as its enthusiasm for the European revolutions of 1848."[1] His poems often appeal directly, and passionately, to the political impulses of his readers, but they do so in ways that do not date. Whitman is always our contemporary, always a beacon. His light beckons us to remember how we constitute a single body, physical and national. We cannot divide ourselves into "us" and "them" but should muck together in the great experience of life. And we must not neglect those in need, those who suffer at the margins of society, the poor, the enslaved, the wounded, the jailed, the dying. Whitman himself did not ignore them, for instance during the Civil War, when he moved from bed to bed in reeking hospital tents, comforting and assisting wounded soldiers. In Whitman, words became deeds.

Dickinson did not have Whitman's robust sense of speaking for a nation, nor did she have his expansive personality. A woman in her time could hardly believe it was her place to become a representative voice. The sexual politics of the nineteenth century in the United States were such that she could not even assume that her voice would be heard at all. Dickinson's poems were invisible to the public during her lifetime (she published only a handful, in local newspapers), and she could never have foreseen the vast posthumous interest in her work. "I'm Nobody," she declares, with typical bluntness, in one poem. Born into a world where the Puritan tradition pulled a veil over women of genius, she had to reformulate herself, creating a poetry of canny subversion ruled by irony and indirection. "Tell all the truth," she cautions herself, "but tell it Slant." Her friend Thomas Wentworth Higginson once referred to her as "my partially cracked poetess at

Amherst." He probably never said this to her face, but he certainly showed some hesitation in the face of her "spasmodic" rhythms and odd mental associations and juxtapositions. She responded forcefully to such criticisms, writing even in her prose with those dashes that she loved: "You think my gait 'spasmodic'—I am in danger—Sir—You think me 'uncontrolled'—I have no Tribunal." This was true: she had no Tribunal but her sovereign imagination, and she defied conventions, expressing her pain, her outrage, her desire, in a most unbridled fashion that was unbecoming to a lady.[2]

The work of poets, according to Dickinson, was to "light but Lamps" and then "go out" themselves. She considered each age "a Lens / Disseminating their / Circumference—." Poets light a lamp and fade away themselves, while the age picks up these beams of light and spreads them around according to the shape and quality of the lens. To a degree, Dickinson acknowledges that each age must take the words of poets and make of them what they will, within the context of the period in which the words were written. A future age may well apply its defining lens (and code of morality) to the same words and find other meanings. Dickinson lit her lamps, creating a vast city of lights in her poetry, and their brightness has not diminished.

Langston Hughes was a poet who spoke up for his African American heritage in a bold and singular fashion. He was not, like Frost or even Whitman or Dickinson, a poet who traded heavily in ambiguity. Few poets have written with such an uncompromising political energy or directness, or with such a sense of deep and unmitigated grievance. In "Dinner Guest: Me," he says: "I know I am / The Negro Problem." In the blistering "Un-American Investigators," he observes that "The committee's fat, / Smug." He suggests bluntly, even crudely, that "The committee shivers / With delight in / Its manure." His biting poem about the Ku Klux Klan concludes:

A klansman said, "Nigger,
Look me in the face—
And tell me you believe in
The great white race."

Of his black brothers and sisters, he writes in a poem called "Warning":

Negroes,
Sweet and docile,
Meek, humble, and kind:
Beware the day
They change their mind!

His indictment of racism in America is nothing less than ferocious. Hughes takes no prisoners, and will protect nobody's feelings. It would have been difficult, even impossible, to discuss Langston Hughes in the White House and ignore his political message. In his case, the message was the medium itself, the point of its existence. He wanted to drop bombs in the streets of polite discourse, and he did so effectively.

Hughes rarely ventured outside the realm of politics and morality, if these may be defined in poetry as a tendency in the poet to address issues of power and to highlight injustice. Repeatedly he asks: How is it possible for a large segment of the American population to live with the promise of liberty when that liberty comes at such a slow pace, with so many reservations? That question recurs in his work from start to finish, assuming many different forms. He takes it upon himself to speak up for the civil rights he regarded as his birthright, and the birthright of other African Americans; his voice is both defiant and beautiful in its presumptions. It has not stopped ringing in our ears.

The question of what right poets have to speak up for anyone at all is complicated. I would defend poets and their right to speak on the simplest grounds, arguing that poets are people who have spent a lot of time thinking about the connection between words and things; they know something about language and its proper applications and directions. Often they feel a sense of responsibility when it comes to speech and are troubled when it seems insufficient to the realities around them. In "Of Modern Poetry," Stevens (who stayed out of most direct political arguments) considers the poet's mandate explicitly. The modern poem, he argues, has to "be living." It has to "face the men of the time and to meet / The women of the time. It has to think about war / And it has to find what will suffice." In the period when Stevens was writing this, during World War II, the poet had to address this terrible conflict (which left sixty million dead in its wake) in some fashion or risk irrelevance. Stevens understood this, and alluded frequently—though with indirection—to war and human conflict in his poems, seeking what he refers to in the final lines of "Notes Toward a Supreme Fiction" as "the bread of faithful speech."

In creating this faithful speech and discovering "what will suffice," poets have no choice but to listen and watch closely, making judgments that will have political and moral ramifications. Whatever their party affiliations, poets have usually been sensitive to their own times, responsive to the cruelties, injustices, and absurdities that confront them, willing to risk taking a position, however nuanced and private, even though they also seem to wish they could turn inward and cultivate their own aesthetic garden. (Voltaire, who talked about the wish to cultivate his own garden, was himself a poet who could not, despite his own wishes, stay out of politics. He became one of the first champions of human rights, insisting on free speech, condemning torture and narrow-mindedness, speaking truth to power again and again—and risking his own neck in the process. Indeed, his latter years were spent in somewhat anxious exile on his estate at Ferney.)

In "North American Time," Adrienne Rich writes about the impossibility of staying "outside" politics. She says, "try telling yourself / you are not accountable / to the life of your tribe / the breath of your planet." She says that you, the poet, are responsible for the breath of your planet, and you simply cannot pretend that "your time does not exist." That would be to cultivate a sense of unreality, to evade responsibility. In a similar vein, in "Views from a Train," Charles Simic looks from the window of his carriage in some unnamed, impoverished country to witness a scene of hideous poverty:

There was the sight of squatters' shacks,
Naked children and lean dogs running

On what looked like a town dump,
The smallest one hopping after them on crutches.

As Simic implies, the poet has to bear witness, to see what is
there, and to express this vision in palpable language. Descrip-
tion becomes a form of revelation, to paraphrase Stevens. Poets
are not in the business of offering solutions, however, although
they sometimes put a utopian vision before the reader, as did
William Blake in "And did those feet?" which ends on this note
of resolution:

I will not cease from mental fight,
Nor shall my sword sleep in my hand,
Till we have built Jerusalem,
In England's green and pleasant land.

This is a tall order, to build Jerusalem—a symbol here of the just
and perfect city. For the most part, poets have done their job
properly if they simply note what is happening around them in
a fresh, true way, in language that neither distorts nor covers over
the situation. For the most part, they need only ask the appro-
priate question, as in "Harlem," by Langston Hughes, where the
poet asks, "What happens to a dream deferred?" Need he say more?

Above all, poets must be held responsible for the speech if not
the life of their tribe, for they are the custodians of language. It
has always been part of their job description to point to things
wrong and right about the human condition, to celebrate and to
condemn as well. A poet's way of saying may have few listeners,
but those who listen do so acutely, and the words of true poems

cut deep and resonate down the decades. They become the bed-rock language of each time and place, a form of meditated speech against which all other language must measure itself.

A few caveats here will be useful to bear in mind as we think about poetry and politics—a complex subject that is easily mis-understood. While poetry often addresses political issues, it would nevertheless be naive to suggest that many poems over the cen-turies have anything overtly political about them. I often recall the brilliant lines from W. H. Auden's elegy for William Butler Yeats, where he writes about the place of poetry in the political and economic marketplace. It is useless, he argues, to imagine big results on the ground from poetic practice:

> For poetry makes nothing happen: it survives
> In the valley of its making where executives
> Would never want to tamper, flows on south
> From ranches of isolation and the busy griefs,
> Raw towns that we believe and die in; it survives,
> A way of happening, a mouth.

Poetry is a "mouth," a speaking voice, and the "mouth" of a river as well, a place where language "comes out." It makes "noth-ing" happen in literal terms: no bridges are built, no wars con-cluded, no energy prices contained. But it survives, and in its survival the race itself survives, having found a mouth, a way of meeting the times with a language adequate to the experience of the times. In "September 1, 1939," Auden writes: "All I have is a voice / To undo the folded lie." This is no small thing in this voiceless, violent world where, as Yeats once observed, "The best lack all conviction, while the worst / Are full of passionate intensity."

Poets obsessively attempt to "undo the folded lie." They write about poverty and war, about the degradation of the environment, about human losses large and small. And they celebrate the daily activities that make life possible in a difficult world. A great deal of "protest poetry"—of yesterday, today, and probably tomorrow—is silly and ineffectual. But a few deeply considered voices always arise in the tradition of the bard, those poets who manage to find words that marry political concerns with poetic practice. It is a tradition that Edmund Spenser, a major poet during the reign of Elizabeth I, described in memorable terms in "A View of the Present State of Ireland" (1596). Spenser was living in Ireland, part of the English occupying force remanded there, and he noted with intense interest that there were "amongst the Irish a certain kind of people called Bards." He said that their profession was "to set forth the praises and dispraises of men in their Poems and Rhymes." The English invasion of Ireland was extremely repressive in the sixteenth century, and these bards were part of the local resistance; indeed, their words rang down the centuries, and their stance gave courage to many who, in later decades, worked for the liberation of Ireland from Britain.[3]

One often finds poets in particularly repressive political cultures taking on these bardic roles. Along these lines, one thinks of Anna Akhmatova in the Soviet Union during the terrible years of Stalin, or Breyten Breytenbach in South Africa during the years of apartheid. These poets stood out as singular and defiant voices of resistance; they themselves became sites of political power, places where morality—at least in language—could find a home.

In times of war, in particular, poets have often spoken up, celebrating the heroism of soldiers in combat, as Tennyson did in "The Charge of the Light Brigade," or, more typically, marking the futility and waste of armed conflict. I think of the gritty, realistic war poems of soldier-poets like Wilfred Owen and Isaac Rosenberg, both of whom wrote passionately about the absurdity of combat in the Great War. The American poet e. e. cummings was also a soldier in that war, and he later wrote a marvelous antiwar poem called "i sing of Olaf glad and big." In that memorable poem he lauds a conscientious objector "whose warmest heart recoiled at war." One might also recall the antiwar stance of poets such as Robert Bly, Adrienne Rich, Daniel Berrigan, Denise Levertov, Allen Ginsberg, and Robert Lowell, each of whom resisted the Vietnam War in various ways. (During World War II, Lowell was a conscientious objector, and he spent time in prison: an experience recorded in one of his best poems, "Memories of West Street and Lepke.") In their lives as well as in their poems, these poets challenged readers to sit up and take notice. They presented a counterbalance to the political rhetoric of the day.

There is a place where poetry, politics, and morality converge, but it will necessarily be a zone of complexity and considerable nuance. Poetry at its best represents a frank, pained, sometimes elated expression of reality. It discovers and contemplates injustice. It laments poverty: the poverty of imagination as well as physical poverty. It asks readers to imagine what has happened and to imagine what might follow from certain actions. Poetry matters because it takes into account the full range of moral considerations, moving against the easy black-and-white formulations that may sound effective in political rhetoric but which cannot, finally, satisfy our deepest needs for a language adequate to the emotional and intellectual range of our experience.

8 a natural world

There is always an analogy between nature and the imagination, and possibly poetry is merely the strange rhetoric of that parallel.

WALLACE STEVENS

Before we move from recklessness to responsibility, from selfishness to a decent happiness, we must want to save our world. And in order to want to save our world we must learn to love it—and in order to love it we must become familiar with it again. That is where my work begins, and why I keep walking, and looking.

MARY OLIVER

It is not the moon, I tell you.
It is these flowers
lighting the yard.

LOUISE GLÜCK

I shall consider the connections between poetry and nature, assuming (as I do) that nature—the wild, good earth that we feed off and that sustains us in spiritual as well as physical ways—matters a great deal. In this vein, poetry is useful because it draws us closer to the earth, helping us to see what lies about us and to understand the philosophical, psychological, and spiritual dimensions of nature. Poetry becomes, in effect, a natural scripture, one that calls us back to the ground itself, with all the physical and metaphorical resonances contained in that phrase.

Poets have usually respected, if not loved, nature, a response that goes back to the pastoral verse of Greek and Roman poetry. This is "nature poetry" in its most traditional form, and it persists to this day, although it is a complex and highly conventional mode with many antithetical elements. In the classical era, poems that we call pastoral or bucolic were set in rural areas and conveyed an idealized sense of nature, which occupied a world very much in contrast to civilized society. The poems that Theocritus and Virgil wrote for their Greek and Roman contemporaries featured a fairly set cast of stylized characters who worked as shepherds. To paraphrase Milton, they warbled their native wood-notes wild in pastures, where nature was inoffensive and gentle, conducive to thoughts of love and feelings of serenity. In this controlled atmosphere, the grass was always green, the sky blue, the midnight starry.

These gentle, often seductive, poems were certainly not written for illiterate farmers; they were composed by extremely intelligent craftsmen, poets who knew the metrical forms of bucolic verse and who understood the conventions of the genre, which they manipulated in subtle ways to amuse sophisticated audiences who longed for simpler times and natural settings (while sitting in their well-appointed houses in Athens or Rome). Needless to say, the natural settings described in these poems existed far away from the hurly-burly of the urban centers where the readers of these poems lived.

There was also a subtle (even hidden) political aspect to this nature writing. The pastoral poet, as William Empson has wisely observed, sought to reestablish a bit of fellow-feeling with rural people: "The essential trick of the old pastoral, which was felt to imply a beautiful relation between rich and poor, was to make simple people express strong feelings (felt as the most universal subject, something fundamentally true about everybody) in learned and fashionable language (so that you wrote about the best subject in the best way). From seeing the two sorts of people combined like this you thought better of both; the best parts of both were used. The effect was in some degree to combine in the reader or author the merits of the two sorts; he was made to mirror in himself more completely the effective elements of the society he lived in."[1]

So pastoral poetry was not simply "nature poetry"; it was about human beings of a particular class within a rural setting.

From this tradition arose variations on a theme, and there were few major poems that did not, in some way, include some aspect of pastoral verse. Chaucer, Milton, and Shakespeare were deeply influenced by the genre of pastoral writing. Romantic poetry from Blake and Wordsworth through the Victorians (Matthew Arnold, Tennyson) rang endless changes on the pastoral mode, raising the genre to new levels. In modern times, one sees poets from Frost and Robinson Jeffers through Gary Snyder, Louise Glück, and Mary Oliver writing about the natural world in ways that might be called pastoral, although the old-fashioned idealized world of nature has given way, in modern writing, to a more complicated setting. Wendell Berry has thought long and hard about the pastoral mode, and has revised our sense of it considerably. Even the so-called "confessional poets," including Robert Lowell and Sylvia Plath among others, performed their acts of self-interrogation (even self-laceration) against a vivid backdrop of nature, which was often viewed in starkly beautiful terms, as when Plath writes about poppies.

Berry is worth thinking about closely. He was himself the child of Kentucky farmers, learning as a boy how to operate a horse-drawn plow. He went off to the city to study, got his graduate degrees in literature, and taught for a while at a university; but he was unhappy there and returned to farm and write in his boyhood setting. His story reminds one of the ancient pastoral poets who left their country settings to take up sophisticated ways in the capital, where they wrote learned poems about rural people for an educated audience. Berry has observed that what happens when rural-based writers go to the city is that they learn to disparage rural things and to denigrate farming as a way of life. He himself refuses to romanticize pastoral life or farming. He knows that it costs a great deal, in human sweat and tears, to farm on a small scale, husbanding the land in a responsible way. But in his poetry and fiction he demonstrates an allegiance to the land itself, and to farm labor, that is heartening. He understands that the memory of the land, in the human mind, is important, and his writing is a means of recovery. As he says in one early essay: "A farmer's relation to his land is the basic and central connection in the relation of humanity to the creation; the agricultural relation *stands for* the large relation. Similarly, marriage is the basic and central community tie; it begins and stands for the relation we have to family and to the larger circles of human association. And these relationships to the creation and to the human community are in turn basic to, and may stand for, our relationship to God—or to the sustaining mysteries and powers of the creation."[2]

This is bracing stuff, deeply conservative in impulse, though gifted with the freedom of liberal thought. His work is conservative in the best sense: it celebrates tradition and looks for what works in that tradition. It looks for health and well-being. It discourages waste and fraud. In his advocacy of the small farm, for example, he has been a vigorous opponent of "agribusiness," aware that what is lost in farming on a large scale is a sense of community. He also understands that farming on a massive or industrial scale is destructive of the topsoil, which is in no way "conservative." Nor is the clear-cutting of large forest tracts conservative. Nor is drilling for oil in wilderness regions. Berry has, again and again, come to the defense of the environment, which he regards as a human environment as well as a place of wildness.

In "A Secular Pilgrimage," Berry meditates on one of the central issues for poetry in our time. "The poetry of this century," he writes, "like the world in this century, has suffered from the schism in the modern consciousness. It has been turned back upon itself, fragmented, obscured in its sense of its function. Like all other human pursuits, it has had to suffer, and to some extent enact, the modern crisis: the failure of the past to teach us to deal with the present or to envision and prepare for a desirable future. It has often seemed to lack wholeness and wisdom."[3] This is not to disparage poetry but to suggest that the field is complex, with successes and failures. Poets are human beings, and they cannot escape the problems of their time or see through all the blind spots. While some poets have been prophets—Blake and Whitman are primary examples—most are workaday creatures who labor in the vineyards, digging their rows, planting seeds, watering the plants, harvesting what they can.

What Berry describes as "the schism in modern consciousness" was defined early in the twentieth century by one of its most vibrant philosophers, Alfred North Whitehead, who argues in *Science and the Modern World* (1925) that human beings have become alienated, in large part, because of "the enormous success of scientific abstraction," which, in the wake of the scientific revolution of the seventeenth century, succeeded in removing the beauty, the sense of wonder, from creation itself. Whitehead points to "a divorce of science from the affirmations of our aesthetic and ethical experiences."[4] Poetry, with its relentless concreteness and affectionate attendance on the natural world, plays a role in the act of restoration, giving back to readers a vision of creation in all its many dimensions.

"Man is the broken giant," writes Emerson in "History" (1841) "and in all his weakness both his body and his mind are invigorated by habits of conversation with nature."[5] This "conversation with nature" has been a basic fact of poetic practice from the earliest times. Chaucer, for example, cannot even get his pilgrims on their way in his Prologue to *The Canterbury Tales* without celebrating the wonders of the "holt and heeth" in springtime, with its April showers and sweet breath of the wind, the tender crops, the melodious birds of the air:

> Whan that Aprill, with his shoures soote
> The droghte of March hath perced to the roote
> And bathed every veyne in swich licour,
> Of which vertu engendred is the flour;
> Whan Zephirus eek with his sweete breeth
> Inspired hath in every holt and heeth
> The tendre croppes, and the yonge sonne
> Hath in the Ram his halfe cours yronne,
> And smale foweles maken melodye,
> That slepen al the nyght with open eye—
> (So priketh hem Nature in hir corages);
> Thanne longen folk to goon on pilgrimages.

English poetry could well be seen as a continuous meditation on the natural world, with its delights and powers of refreshments, its beckoning of the reader to a sense of spiritual keenness. Shakespeare, the boy from Warwickshire, could hardly dampen his enthusiasm for nature, as celebrated in the forest of Arden. The exiled duke in *As You Like It* seems hardly to suffer from his loss of contact with civilization, for example. "Are not these woods / More free from peril than the envious court?" he asks. Even the seasonal winds and rains appear to strip away false things; they are "counselors / That feelingly persuade me what I am." Far from feeling cut off from sources of knowledge and power, the duke finds "tongues in trees, books in running brooks, / Sermons in stones, and good in everything" (II, i). All human speech is measured against the vast silence of the woods, as the wise fool Touchstone suggests when he comments: "You have said, but whether wisely or no, let the forest judge" (III, ii).

Poetry is a response to silence, even the result of its cultivation. It is, as Jorie Graham writes in "Self-Portrait as the Gesture Between Them": "The rip in the fabric where the action begins, the opening of the narrow passage." And where better to cultivate this silence than in nature, where the mind settles against a particular landscape, finds deep sustenance in beauty, feels the hardness of the earth, the balance that comes from walking in close contact with the world? Poets have provided excellent field guides to particular natural settings. One could do worse, when strolling in the pastures of Warwickshire, than to have Shakespeare in hand, the author who wrote in *Troilus and Cressida*: "One touch of nature makes the whole world kin." His imagery is usually drawn from his boyhood region, which gave him his grounding. Even when he writes about some imaginary place, such as the forest of Arden, he is writing about his native county, evoking its flora and fauna, its light, its moderate weather and yielding pastoral landscape. One could, in a similar vein, turn to the poems of Andrew Marvell, Henry Vaughan, George Herbert, William Wordsworth, and countless others to learn about the English countryside. In the nineteenth century, one could find no more vivid celebrants of nature than Gerard Manley Hopkins, the Jesuit priest whose work offers a fresh theology of nature, and Walt Whitman, who drank from the dark pools of Emersonian philosophy.

Hopkins is fascinating, for he developed a natural theology of sorts, one that combines Christian elements with an almost pagan sense of nature's power to invade and involve, even to embody (or make manifest) the spirit. He kept a journal, where in sensuous detail he records the images that strike him on his walks. On May 9, 1871, for instance, he writes about "bluebells in the little wood between the College and the highroad and in one of the Hurst Green cloughs." He notes with elaborate precision: "In the little wood opposite the light they stood in blackish spreads or sheddings like the spots on a snake. The heads are then like thongs and solemn in grain and grape-colour. But in the clough through the light they came in falls of sky-colour washing the brows and slacks of the ground with vein-blue, thickening at the double, vertical themselves and the young grass and brake fern combed vertical, but the brake struck the upright of all this and light winged transoms. It was a lovely sight."[6]

Taken together, his poems represent a paean to the natural world. "Glory be to God for dappled things," he writes in "Pied Beauty," evoking a landscape that is "plotted and pieced," filled with "dappled" cows, trout, finches' wings, and so many other things. His sense of nature is pervasively theologized; it is the strenuous power of God in operation that he discovers behind the amazing variety and strength of beauty, as in "Hurrahing in Harvest," where he says: "I walk, I lift up, I lift up heart, eyes, / Down all that glory in the heavens to glean our Saviour." In "Spring," he celebrates in pagan (almost pantheistic) fashion a scene that would have seemed familiar to Theocritus or Virgil:

> Nothing is so beautiful as Spring—
>> When weeds, in wheels, shoot long and lovely and lush;
>> Thrush's eggs look little low heavens, and thrush
> Through the echoing timber does so rinse and wring
> The ear, it strikes like lightnings to hear him sing;
>> The glassy peartree leaves and blooms, they brush
>> The descending blue; that blue is all in a rush
> With richness; the racing lambs too have fair their fling.

But he rapidly questions the source of such inspiration: "What is all this juice and all this joy?" He sees in this pastoral scene a "strain of the earth's sweet being in the beginning / In Eden garden." In other words, God offers these glimmering scenes to remind us of what we have lost and what is to be gained through faith. Hopkins ends by praising Christ: "O maid's child." Nature is, indeed, a symbol of the spirit for Hopkins, and his landscapes brim with that spirit, overflow with grace. Christ, for him, is everywhere, even within the least of things, as well as the sum of all parts.

Hopkins responded powerfully to Whitman, in whom he found a kindred spirit (although he shrank from the overt homoerotic feelings that Whitman expressed in certain passages). One can hardly open *Leaves of Grass,* Whitman's vast (in every sense) collection of poems, without finding countless strange, marvelous evocations of nature. A few gleanings follow:

Roots and leaves themselves alone are these,
Scents brought to men and women from the wild woods and
   pond-side,
Breast-sorrel and pinks of love, fingers that wind around tighter
   than vines,
Gushes from the throats of birds hid in the foliage of trees as the
   sun is risen. ["Roots and leaves themselves alone"]

I saw in Louisiana a live-oak growing,
All alone stood it and the moss hung down from the branches,
Without any companion it grew there uttering joyous leaves of
   dark green. ["I Saw in Louisiana a live-oak growing"]

The earth, that is sufficient,
I do not want the constellations any nearer,
I know they are very well where they are,
I know they suffice for those who belong to them. ["Song of the
   Open Road"]

O to have been brought up on bays, lagoons, creeks, or along the
   coast,
To continue and be employ'd there all my life,
The briny and damp smell, the shore, the salt weeds exposed at
   low water. ["A Song of Joys"]

I swear the earth shall surely be complete to him or her who shall
   be complete,
The earth remains jagged and broken only to him or her who
   remains jagged and broken. ["A Song of the Rolling Earth"]

I stand as on some mighty eagle's beak,
Eastward the sea absorbing, viewing (nothing but sea and sky),

> The tossing waves, the foam, the ships in the distance,
> The wild unrest, the snowy, curling caps—that inbound urge and
>   urge of waves,
> Seeking the shores forever. ["From Montauk Point"]

Whitman allowed the world to ravish his eye, and so natural images abound in the poems, often turned into analogies. He searches the human soul, which he finds embodied in natural surroundings. At times, he himself becomes a blade of grass, a breeze, a tree. His feelings roll toward the shoreline, like the waves in "From Montauk Point." His entire philosophy of spirit in nature finds apt, even perfect, expression in the glorious finale of *Song of Myself.* The soul of the poet, he suggests, will always be found precisely where he says to look for it:

> The spotted hawk swoops by and accuses me, he complains of my
>   gab and my loitering.
>
> I too am not a bit tamed, I too am untranslatable,
> I sound my barbaric yawp over the roofs of the world.
>
> The last scud of day holds back for me,
> It flings my likeness after the rest and true as any on the shadow'd
>   wilds,
> It coaxes me to the vapor and the dusk.
>
> I depart as air, I shake my white locks at the runaway sun,
> I effuse my flesh in eddies, and drift it in lacy jags.
>
> I bequeath myself to the dirt to grow from the grass I love,
> If you want me again look for me under your boot-soles.
>
> You will hardly know who I am or what I mean,
> But I shall be good health to you nevertheless,
> And filter and fibre your blood.

Failing to fetch me at first keep encouraged,
Missing me one place search another,
I stop somewhere waiting for you.

. . . . .

Poets re-ground themselves in the natural world, inhabiting a paradise of signs and symbols that moves beyond the reductive dualism that puts science and technology on one side of a divide, the arts and humanities on the other. In a way, with its regard for concrete reality, poetry may well serve as an essential bridge between the arts and sciences, as John Elder suggests in *Imagining the Earth* (1985), a seminal study of poetry and its relation to nature. Elder describes the impoverishment of human beings in their alienation from the natural world and sees poetry as essential in the process of recovery: "To start from the soil again is the task when human culture has become impoverished. A poetry that draws its nourishment from rootedness in a chosen spot defines the interchange of past and present through that spot's own cycle of renewing surrender and inheritance. And tradition thus comes to be measured against the most pragmatic of criteria: will it grow here, will it enrich this field? A broad awareness of culture and poetry is useful to a person in the same way that his or her natural responsiveness is enhanced by knowing the basic principles of ecology."[7]

We come, ideally, to a vision of nature that includes humankind in its capacious fold and has a spiritual as well as an ethical dimension. In fact, poets have been doing this from the start, grounding their work in a specific place and time, evoking that place in concrete terms, allowing meaning to inhere as language finds a verbal equivalency of sorts, one that gestures movingly in the direction of natural beauty. The poet becomes, as Emerson suggests, a figure like Adam, the namer in the garden of Eden, amazed by his own powers of observation if somewhat unsettled by the difficulty of looking through nature or beyond it: a crisis depicted by Milton in *Paradise Lost* (IV), where Eve approaches a pellucid lake:

> I thither went
> With unexperienc't thought, and laid me down
> On the green bank, to look into the clear
> Smooth Lake, that to me seem'd another Sky.
> As I bent down to look, just opposite,
> A Shape within the watr'y gleam appear'd
> Bending to look on me, I started back,
> It started back, but pleas'd I soon return'd,
> Pleas'd it return'd as soon with answering looks
> Of sympathy and love; there I had fixt
> Mine eyes till now, and pin'd with vain desire.

Nature becomes a mirror that flatters the viewer, exciting vain desires that cannot be fulfilled. One looks into this shimmering thing with the hope of seeing through it to something beyond, but—just as often—finds oneself, a point that Frost wrestles with in "For Once, Then, Something."

Frost remains, among the modern poets, the preeminent maker of pastoral verse. But this tradition is complex (as Empson suggests), with social as well as philosophical bearings. John F. Lynen puts it well: "The kind of poetry Frost writes can best be understood by observing the method by which he has sought to make the present moment represent all other times, and the particular place he describes, the human situation as it has always existed. His essential technique is that of the pastoral. He has explored wide and manifold ranges of being by viewing reality within the mirror of the natural and unchanging world of rural life. Pastoralism, whether in Frost or in the poets of the Arcadian tradition, will always at first appear to involve an escape from the world as we know it, but actually it is an exploration upstream, past the city with its riverside factories and shipping, on against the current of time and change to the clear waters of the source."[8]

In "Directive," a late poem of extraordinary power, Frost gathers the wisdom of a lifetime in poetry. He begins by taking us back in time, back into nature itself: "Back in a time made simple by the loss / Of detail." The poem "directs" us into the woods, to an earlier, more rustic, time; but there is no hint of sentimentality here. This earlier time is only made "simple" by the loss of detail, "like graveyard marble sculpture in the weather." If one lived in that earlier time, one would have to confront the manifold hardships of that era: smallpox, a lack of modern tools, long hours at work, and so forth. The idylls of Theocritus and Virgil are not exactly Frost's idea of the pasture, as he locates his farmers (and himself) in the rocky pastureland of northern New England, where life was hard. (Frost was himself a farmer in his earlier decades, near Derry, New Hampshire, and he experienced the poverty of this situation at first hand.)

"Directive" is Frost's answer to Eliot's *Waste Land*. He too finds something of value in tradition: the tradition of pastoral. And he plays that tradition like a violin, plucking the whole range of notes, adding his own harsh and melancholy tones—thus criticizing and modifying the tradition at the same time. In the blasted landscape of modern times, when so much has been lost, and humankind so alienated by attitudes that Whitehead and Berry, among others, have located in the scientific materialism that removes anything human, ethical, or spiritual from the natural world, Frost rediscovers value in that same natural world. "Your destination and your destiny's / A brook that was the water of the house," he informs us. That brook is "Cold as a spring as yet so near its source, / Too lofty and original to rage." This might well describe Frost's poetry, which is a living stream, lofty and original but quiet, not raging. In the fetching last lines, he says: "Here are your waters and your watering place. / Drink and be whole again beyond confusion."

Recall that Frost defined poetry as "a momentary stay against confusion." Life is most often a form of confusion. Only in the moment of the poem, within its steady unfolding of a vision, does life clarify. One sees "something," for once. That such moments of vision, however fleeting, occur in the woods is not accidental. For Frost, like Emerson (his true mentor), and so many poets before him going back to Shakespeare and Chaucer, the natural world is a place of refreshment, a kindred setting, where the soul finds lodging in the imagery at hand, where the spirit is cloaked and (in the best sense of that term) revealed. "All revelation has been ours," Frost writes elsewhere, in "Revelation." And, at times, we might agree.

"As a poet I hold the most archaic values on earth," wrote Gary Snyder. "They go back to the upper Paleolithic: the fertility of the soil, the magic of animals, the power-vision in solitude, the terrifying initiation and rebirth, the love and ecstasy of the dance, the common work of the tribe." Poets continue to examine the natural world closely, reading spirit in nature, finding analogies in natural images, celebrating wilderness as well as more humanized natural settings. Among the prominent American poets who have read the natural world closely in the past few decades are A. R. Ammons, Ruth Stone, Adrienne Rich, Robert Bly, Wendell Berry, Anne Stevenson, Mary Oliver, Charles Wright, Louise Glück, Jorie Graham, Ellen Bryant Voigt, Robert Hass, and Mary Jo Salter. One finds a wide range of approaches to nature in this work, as Bernard W. Quetchenbach notes in *Back from the Far Field* (2000), his useful study of American nature poetry in the late twentieth century. These poets have "laid groundwork for an art that could help restore humanity's membership in the natural community of the earth," he says. "That would clearly be a poetry that matters."[9]

Charles Wright and Mary Oliver have each shown a particular dedication to what might be called the realities of nature, including its daily flux. Both are Emersonian in the broadest sense, in that they read nature as a symbol of the spirit; but they embody the world in their poetry in immensely particular ways, finding a distinct language and angle of vision to bring the reader closer to the natural world.

In *A Short History of the Shadow* (2002), his fifteenth collection, Wright revisits "Old fires / old geographies," as he says in "Looking Around." Many of the poems here resemble in form and texture those of his middle period, as represented in *The*

World of the Ten Thousand Things: Poems, 1980–1990. In that work, the terse, imagistic lyrics of his earlier verse gave way to long and languid meditations in the loose, associative format of a journal. Now as then, Wright centers each poem in a particular place (Tennessee, Virginia, California, Italy), sometimes skipping blithely from landscape to landscape, season to season. He addresses large matters: the place of human intelligence in nature, the nature and role of memory and time in the life of the soul, the fate of language as a conduit between spirit and matter. Wright has been, in a sense, adding apocryphal books to his own hermetic scripture with each poem for many years.

Admitting to a "thirst for the divine" in "Lost Language," he catalogues his habits and desires:

> I have a hankering for the dust-light, for all things illegible.
> I want to settle myself
> Where the river falls on hard rocks,
>
> where no one can cross,
> Where the star-shadowed, star-colored city lies, just out of reach.

A dark Emersonian, Wright reads the book of Nature closely, fetching the reader's attention with compelling aphorisms, phrases arranged to create a subtle, alluring music. He could not be mistaken for any other poet, although one notices the remnants of his reading, thoroughly absorbed and transmogrified, in almost every line. It's often amusing to hear him echoing Whitman, Eliot, or Stevens. When he says, for example, "I like it out here" in "Why, It's as Pretty as a Picture," one can't help but hear Stevens's similar remark in "The Motive for Metaphor." Of course, poems often unfold from poems, and most good literature is pervasively allusive, building on the language of previous poetry. Wright knows this; indeed, he embraces it, shrugging off any "anxiety of influence."

Though rooted in the traditions of European and American Romanticism, Wright has kept an eye on the East and its traditions of spirituality, most vividly in *China Trace* (1977). In his later poems as well he alludes easily and often to Chinese poets and philosophers, who embrace the concept of emptiness in ways that complement Wright's aesthetic, as he suggests in the gorgeous "Body and Soul II," where he presents another in his series of poems in the ars poetica mode:

> Every true poem is a spark,
> and aspires to the condition of the original fire
> Arising out of the emptiness.
> It is that same emptiness it wants to reignite.
> It is that same engendering it wants to be re-engendered by.

In "Body and Soul" itself, Wright embraces his aesthetic more ardently than anywhere in his previous writing, saying:

> I used to think the power of words was inexhaustible,
> That how we said the world
> was how it was, and how it would be.
> I used to imagine that word-sway and word-thunder
> Would silence the Silence and all that,
> That words were the Word,
> That language could lead us inexplicably to grace,
> As though it were geographical.
> I used to think these things when I was young.
> I still do.

Movingly, Wright places his confidence in the gnostic way of knowledge, in the appropriation of logos through language itself, in "word-sway and word-thunder," a formulation that recalls Hopkins, who sought the divine in language, wherein he discovered an "inscape" (his term for a distinct internal form) that embodied the mystery of grace. Wright is a seer in the truest sense. His vatic stance, though unpretentious because the manner of the poet is often offhand and colloquial, remains central to the meaning of his work, which falls smack in the line of American visionary poetry.

Much the same could be said for Mary Oliver, who has published more than fifteen collections since 1963. She has shown astonishing consistency, separating herself from the Romantic tradition of nature poetry in her own way while adding yet another layer of complexity. Even Wordsworth, as Janet McNew observes, "demoted nature from mother to 'homely nurse' because he wanted to claim a more diverse parentage, a patriarchal one with 'God, who is our home.'" (There is a good point here, though McNew traces only one line of thought in Wordsworth; another occurs in *The Prelude* and in many of his sonnets, where he longs to become a pagan and lose himself in the folds of nature, which he sees as encompassing all living creatures.) Oliver certainly refuses to separate herself, as a creature, from other creatures; indeed, she attaches herself vehemently to the natural world as part and parcel of the creation. Her visionary goal "involves constructing a subjectivity that does not depend on separation from a world of objects."[10]

One sees an almost terrifying immersion in nature in books

such as *American Primitive* (1983), her most vivid early work. In those poems she (or the speaker) becomes, in turn, a bear, a whale, or a fish—a shape-shifter, protean, plastic. Like Gary Snyder, she seems to hold "the most archaic values on earth." Indeed, a sense of the land as a sacred domain and repository of memory and myth was part of her vision from the outset, in *No Voyage and Other Poems* (1963).

The full range of her talents occurs in *Blue Iris* (2004). Fittingly, the volume bears a suggestive epigraph from Emerson: "Flowers and fruits are always fit presents; flowers, because they are a proud assertion that a ray of beauty outvalues all the utilities of the world." This gathering of poems and essays evokes a range of vegetable things: morning glories, sunflowers, goldenrod, poppies, skunk cabbages, lilies, the blue iris of the title. Some of the poems recall earlier incarnations of these flowers, as evoked in poems by Sylvia Plath or Theodore Roethke, both of whom found wild but kindred spirits in natural objects, upon which they cast their thoughts with a fierce intensity.

Oliver does not share quite the intensity of Plath or Roethke. She does not, in fact, have anything like the metaphysical intensity of Charles Wright (or, for that matter, Louise Glück, who has written some of the most vivid poems of our time about the natural world). Oliver's is a breezier spirit, although I find her evocations haunting and, often, irresistible. "Attention is the beginning of devotion," she writes in "Upstream," an essay that reads like entries from a journal. Her attention is well focused in several of these poems, such as "Poppies," which invites comparison with such poems as "Death Be Not Proud" by John

Donne or "And death shall have no dominion" by Dylan Thomas. It is a poem that pits life (the poppies, which send up their "orange flares") against death: "There isn't a place / in this world that doesn't / sooner or later drown / in the indigos of darkness." The "black, curved blade" of the Grim Reaper will not be stopped, Oliver suggests; but there is nevertheless "an invitation / to happiness" that can be found in the poppies, in the natural world itself. There is, indeed, "a kind of holiness" that the poet finds "palpable and redemptive." She can hardly contain her joy at the end of this poem:

Inside the bright fields,

Touched by their rough and spongy gold
I am washed and washed
in the river
of earthly delight—

and what are you going to do—
what can you do
about it—
deep, blue night?

9 divine parameters: a reading of *four quartets*

Heaven is not like flying or
    swimming,
but has something to do with
    blackness and a strong glare.

ELIZABETH BISHOP

God is the poetry caught in any
    religion.

LES MURRAY

P oetry is, at its best, a kind of scripture. It represents the inspired language of generations, language that helps us to live our lives by directing us along certain paths. It is not just that poetry matters; *certain* poems matter. I have myself looked to specific poems for inspiration over many decades. As readers of this book could guess, I have been especially fond of poems by Robert Frost, Wallace Stevens, and T. S. Eliot, who are among the great modern poets. Here I look closely at one of my favorite poems, Eliot's *Four Quartets,* as an example of poetry that has helped me to live my life. I'll examine this poem— which is in fact a sequence of interlocking poems—as a kind of spiritual guide.

Readers must, of course, find the poems that matter personally to them: this is the adventure of reading. But I want to recommend Eliot's sequence as a good place to start, for the *Quartets* offers us the deep wisdom of a lifetime spent in contemplation in poetry that draws on many of the world's religions, including Christianity, Buddhism, and Hinduism. It is visionary in the best sense of that overused term, and a work that puts before readers a broad, ecumenical synthesis (although because Eliot was a Christian, the emphasis naturally falls there). Once again, and quite willfully, perhaps, I intend to look at this poem as I always have, as one that offers directions for living. Eliot attempts to answer questions that to me seem basic and compelling: What is the human condition? How do we understand time and our place in the chronological cosmos? Do we have a purpose on this earth? What are the truths that literature and scripture can teach us? (By "scripture" I refer not only to the Bible but to the great tradition of wisdom literature, which Eliot—who studied Sanskrit at Harvard—draws on freely throughout the *Quartets*.) And finally Eliot asks: What role does art have to play in helping us to understand these questions, and to puzzle out answers?

The sequence bears an epigraph, in Greek, that consists of two fragments from Heraclitus, a pre-Socratic philosopher. Let me quote them in English:

> Although the logos is common to everyone, most people behave as though they have a wisdom of their own.
>
> The way up and the way down are the same way.

These enigmatic fragments provide a subtle key to the spiritual meaning of the *Quartets*. In the first, one encounters that complex and untranslatable word *logos*. In the beginning was the word, logos, begins the Gospel of John. This Greek word, often used by Plotinus (a philosopher who drew inspiration from Plato), refers, as it always has, to the core of truth, a sense of deep and ongoing reality, the timeless word that "was God," as John says, "in the beginning," and which persists, outside of time. *Logos* also means "pattern": the eternal pattern of the cosmos. It refs as well to the kingdom of heaven that lies within us. It is freedom from the wheel of life, a concept derived from Hinduism. It is silence, the goal of all poetry, all art, all religious practice. And by religion I refer to that term again in its literal or root sense, *re-ligio,* a "linking back" or reconnection to the logos, the deep pattern, the still center, that eternal moment we *commonly* experience, as Heraclitus suggests, but which we lose in the chatter and bustle of life, as each of us tries foolishly and helplessly to achieve some wisdom of our own, something beyond the obvious and eternal wisdom that remains at hand, within our reach, actually within us.

To revert to a simple cosmology: we look up at the "heavens" for God, for logos, for meaning. And yet we look down as well, Heraclitus suggests. This is of course a spatial metaphor: up and down. But these vertical routes are "the same way." In essence Heraclitus (at least to me) suggests that there are contrary ways to arrive at enlightenment, to discover the silent space within us, to become—in the Christian phrase that has become rather trashy in recent years—saved.

The "way and the truth and the life" that the Gospel writer talks about are really ways and truths and lives, but they all point to one center, one word, *logos.* This may seem obscure, but I hope it will gradually clarify in the context of Eliot's text.

First consider the general shape of each quartet. The term itself, of course, has musical associations, and one sees a distinct melodic structure in each of these five-part sequences. (I would note for the record that the quartet, as developed by Haydn and explored by Beethoven, Bartók, and others, was usually a four-part sequence.) As in a musical quartet, themes in each of Eliot's quartets are established, revisited, and synthesized. The music of poetry was a vivid subject for him: he always composed with melody in mind, as melody is pattern, and a poem may be considered the search for a deep rhythmic and melodic pattern, a kind of speech that, like music itself, speaks past speech.

Another obvious thing about the *Quartets* is that each poem is rooted in a place that possessed autobiographical resonance for Eliot, a place of what he called "significant soil." "Burnt Norton" refers to a house in Gloucestershire that Eliot visited in 1934, and the poem meditates on a visionary or mystical experience in the rose garden of that house. "East Coker" refers to a village in Somerset, from which one of Eliot's ancestors departed for North America in 1669. "The Dry Salvages" is a reference to a cluster of rocks off the coast of Cape Ann, north of Boston, where Eliot spent many holidays as a boy. Finally, "Little Gidding," the fourth quartet, refers to a village in Cambridgeshire that Eliot visited in 1936. It was the site of an Anglican religious community visited by Charles I in 1633; the king returned there in 1646, in flight from anti-royalist government troops, who destroyed the community. In a sense, "Little Gidding" is a poem of restoration, in the broadest sense of that term: the restoration of the monarch and the restoration of the kingdom of God within us.

In each quartet there are five sections. The first is philosophical, though grounded in a particular place and time, as the titles indicate. General themes are established, the way they are in a musical quartet. Words and phrases are put into play, and Eliot returns to them repeatedly, almost liturgically. In the second section, Eliot typically opens with a tightly rhymed, densely symbolical lyric. In the rather prosy second part of each second section, he meditates on the preceding lyric, restating its themes in a more general way. In the third section, Eliot takes the way down, the dark way, the *via negativa* or "dark night of the soul." The imagery of hell frequently recurs, sometimes in the London Underground, a metaphor for living hell. In the fourth section, usually a short lyric of intense darkness and compression, Eliot drops into hell, going deeper and deeper, with hell being defined as a place where God is absent and where the divine pattern of the cosmos cannot be seen or felt. From here, Eliot invariably moves toward the elevated language of the fifth section, which—not unlike the second section—is divided into two parts. In the first, Eliot meditates on the use of art, including poetry and scripture. He writes in a personal way here, with astonishing directness and honesty, standing before us bluntly, in humility and poise. These beautiful parts—always my favorite—lead into the majestic final chorus, the second half of each fifth section, where all the trumpets sound, the flowers open, and themes struck in the first sections are revisited, restated, synthesized.

Eliot wrote "Burnt Norton" as a single independent poem, only later seeing the possibility of a sequence. A visionary experience dominates the first section, set in the rose garden of the abandoned house. The magnificent vision fills a drained pool: "Dry the pool, dry concrete, brown edged." Suddenly the pool is "filled with water out of sunlight," and a lotus flower is manifest: "And the lotus rose, quietly, quietly." This flower becomes "the heart of light." But this vision, like all beatific visions, cannot sustain itself within human time, clock time, the time of seasons and revolutions of the earth. A cloud passes, and the vision fades. Eliot writes, poignantly: "Human kind / cannot bear very much reality." It's a fabulous line, lifted from Eliot's earlier play about a martyred archbishop, *Murder in the Cathedral.* This reality, which necessarily overwhelms humankind, is the reality of God, the reality of unmediated vision. Eliot knows only too well that ordinary men and women cannot hope to dwell in the white heat of that intense light.

In this section Eliot draws on his deep knowledge of Buddhist scriptures, as seen in his reference to the lotus flower, a traditional Eastern symbol of enlightenment. This brings us to another central symbol in this sequence: the tree. This tree is, first, the Bodhi or Bo tree, under which the Buddha sat for seven years before attaining enlightenment. The Bo tree prefigures here the ultimate tree for Eliot, the cross of Christ, embodied in the yew that he refers to later. (The yew is associated with the cross by Christian tradition.) But another tree appears in section 2 of "Burnt Norton," the "bedded axle-tree." This is the deep image at the center of his tightly rhymed, tetrameter lyric in section 2:

Garlic and sapphires in the mud
Clot the bedded axle-tree.
The trilling wire in the blood
Sings below inveterate scars
Appeasing long forgotten wars.

The axle-tree is drawn from Norse mythology, where it is called Yggdrasil, the world tree. In the myth, all creation rises from the roots of this fundamental tree. The world turns around it. Eliot ponders the image in the second half of this section, the prosy part, where he writes about the "still point of the turning world," alluding to the paradox of the wheel: the rim goes round and round, but the axle, the center, remains still. It also refers obliquely to the Hindu wheel of life. This is the point "where past and future are gathered" and where the dance is: an orderly and celebratory dance, which finds its culmination in the next quartet, "East Coker," with its vision of a seventeenth-century village in Somerset, as the inhabitants, hand in hand, dance around a fire: "Keeping time, / Keeping the rhythm in their dancing / As in their living in the living seasons."

From this follows one of Eliot's great catalogues, with its loud verbal echoes of Ecclesiastes:

> The time of the seasons and the constellations
> The time of milking and the time of harvest
> The time of the coupling of man and woman
> And that of beasts. Feet rising and falling.
> Eating and drinking. Dung and death.

What life *should* be like is put before us as the dance of community, the dance of lovers, in the rhythms of the seasons that mirror the seasons of life, all moving around the central fire, a flame that leaps toward heaven: the concluding and summarizing image of *Four Quartets,* as pictured in the final lines of "Little Gidding," where the fire and the rose "are one." This fiery rose (representing the Trinity) is also what Dante encountered in *Paradiso,* the last book of the *Divine Comedy.*

First, however, Eliot escorts us into the dark of section 3, "a place of disaffection." In the London Underground, as in all unholy places in the city, one encounters faces "distracted from distraction by distraction," as Eliot put it so well in "Burnt Norton." Everywhere one sees "Men and bits of paper, whirled by the cold wind." We follow the important men of business and government and culture as they plunge into the Underground: "O dark dark dark. They all go into the dark." Eliot merely quotes here, deftly, lifting a haunting line from Milton's *Samson Agonistes,* summoning a vision of human despair. And so we regard those who live by appetite alone: "The captains, merchant bankers, eminent men of letters," and so forth. No prominence in life allows one to escape from the fact of mortality. Everyone must come to terms with the limits of life, and with its possibilities as well, those "hints and guesses" that point to one end, which is always present: the Eternal Now.

Of course, Eliot is wise enough not to disparage the dark way, as the way down and the way up, as Heraclitus suggested, are the same. This represents a genuine way of knowledge: "You must go by a way which is the way of ignorance," the poet tells us. "In order to possess what you do not possess / You must go by the way of dispossession."

We have all, at times, gone the way of dispossession, lost in our own appetites, burrowing into solitude, taking no hints, making no guesses, shutting out the possibility of light and love. "Human kind / cannot bear very much reality." And so we withdraw, we forget, we refuse to "wait and pray," as the scriptures instruct us, and as Eliot concludes in the fifth part of "The Dry Salvages," in a passage remarkable for its wisdom, its depth and beauty:

> But to apprehend
> The point of intersection of the timeless
> With time, is an occupation for the saint—
> No occupation either, but something given
> And taken, in a lifetime's death in love,
> Ardour and selflessness and self-surrender.
> For most of us, there is only the unattended
> Moment, the moment in and out of time,
> The distraction fit, lost in a shaft of sunlight,
> The wild thyme unseen, or the winter lightning
> Or the waterfall, or music heard so deeply
> That it is not heard at all, but you are the music
> While the music lasts. These are only hints and guesses,
> Hints followed by guesses; and the rest
> Is prayer, observance, discipline, thought and action.

I can't imagine a better prescription for what ails us: Prayer, observance, discipline, thought, and action. Beyond these things, life consists of hints and guesses, and perhaps those unattended moments when we hear something lovely, or smell something odd and memorable, or stumble on a line of poetry that sticks, or meet someone who moves us, or discover in the patterns of nature the lineaments of our own spirit.

I would mark especially the last word in Eliot's prescription: action. "And right action is freedom," he says. Right action leads to "freedom / From past and future." This freedom is the ultimate liberation, betokening release from the wheel of time. Right action must be subject to the individual conscience as well as communal norms. One comes to action last, as Eliot notes, having moved through prayer, observance, discipline, and thought. Without the previous four things, right action is difficult of access, perhaps impossible to discern. And right action, always, occurs in time, as choices are made, paths taken or refused.

Eliot's sense of time is deeply informed by his understanding of Buddhist and Hindu thought, which he alludes to frequently in the *Quartets,* as in the third part of "The Dry Salvages," with a reference to Krishna. In the Eastern tradition, a distinction is made between clock time and eternal time. The first is synchronic time, which moves from tick to tock, down the line, from birth to old age; this is the grid against which our lives unfold in lockstep fashion. On the other hand is eternal time, found at the "still point of the turning world." Eliot works through various concepts of time in the quartets, always moving toward liberation from time, or time as eternal presence, as the perpetual kingdom of God, "a paradise within you, happier far," as Milton wrote in *Paradise Lost.*

What is noteworthy here, and very much Eliot's point, is that human beings cannot evade time. It is our duty to move through it, fastened to the wheel of life. As he writes in the magical final part of "Little Gidding"—

> A people without history
> Is not redeemed from time, for history is a pattern
> Of timeless moments. So, while the light fails

> On a winter's afternoon, in a secluded chapel
> History is now and England.

History is now and England. It is time and place. It is also a pattern of timeless moments, and so Eliot traces those moments in his own life: at the ruined manor house called Burnt Norton, or in Somerset, where in the seventeenth century the Eliot family began its journey from the Old World to the New (where Eliot was born, in Saint Louis, Missouri, only to return to England for good in the early twentieth century, thus completing a circle of sorts). Finally, history is the site of the monastic community of Little Gidding, a place rich in resonance.

Place is crucial for Eliot, and specific places meant a great deal to him. "The Dry Salvages" opens with a river: "I do not know much about gods; but I think that the river / Is a strong brown god." This river represents all rivers—to a degree—but mainly the glorious Mississippi, "conveyor of commerce." The river is useful but "untrustworthy," capable of immense destruction in times of flood. Eliot recalls the presence of this river in his Missouri boyhood:

> His rhythm was present in the nursery bedroom,
> In the rank ailanthus of the April dooryard,
> In the smell of grapes on the autumn table,
> And the evening circle in the winter gaslight.

An astonishing image follows, what literary critics would call a totalizing image, in that so much is gathered into its orbit of meaning: "The river is within us, the sea is all about us."

"The river is within us, the sea is all about us." What we have here is a symbolic representation of time as chronological, as one step after another, in contrast to time as *durée,* to use a word favored by the philosopher Henri Bergson, whose lectures Eliot attended in Paris. The image contrasts time as a line with time as a circle, a perpetual and ever-present loop of reality: the goal of the river, if I may add a touch of teleology. The river stands in for clock time, moving inexorably from source to mouth. It spills into the sea of eternity, is swallowed up, dissolved, as each of us returns to the eternal waters, our first home.

This latter truth, that the river of life ends where it begins, finds its aphoristic expression in "East Coker," where Eliot writes: "In my end is my beginning." This French aphorism was adopted as a motto by Mary, Queen of Scots, another of the several martyrs alluded to by Eliot in the *Quartets.* The obverse of this aphorism, equally true, opens the second quartet: "In my beginning is my end." The poem itself, opening and closing thus, performs a loop, biting its own tail and disappearing, like the mythical world serpent. Just as "Burnt Norton" contemplates the difference between temporal and eternal times, "East Coker" celebrates succession within temporal time as "Houses rise and fall, crumble, are extended, / Are removed, destroyed, restored."

The opening stanza culminates in yet another grand catalogue of examples, once more echoing the language of the King James translation of Ecclesiastes:

Houses live and die: there is a time for building
And a time for living and for generation
And a time for the wind to break the loosened pane

And to shake the wainscot where the field-mouse trots
And to shake the tattered arras woven with a silent motto.

That silent motto was "In my end is my beginning." That is, through the door of death, we enter life, thus substituting the necessary (sometimes beautiful and sometimes arid) time of the clock for the perpetual present, which is ultimate reality: what Eliot glimpses briefly in the garden at Burnt Norton but cannot regard for long, as "human kind / cannot bear very much reality."

To historicize the poem for a moment, we should remember that the first quartet was written in the late thirties, when political storm clouds were darkening the skies of Europe. The last three quartets are war poems, although the war enters at an oblique angle. A friend of mine, a Scottish poet who fought in World War II, has told me about waiting eagerly, even frantically, for each of these quartets to appear. He rushed to buy the brief pamphlets, which offered comfort in a time of darkness. But they contain that darkness as well, demonstrating that the way down and the way up are the same way.

In "Little Gidding," the war emerges in all its literal force. Eliot, himself a fire warden during the London bombings, recalls walking out of the Underground after a night of fiery destruction:

In the uncertain hour before the morning
    Near the ending of interminable night
    At the recurrent end of the unending
After the dark dove with the flickering tongue
    Had passed below the horizon of his homing
    While the dead leaves still rattled on like tin
Over the asphalt where no other sound was

> Between three districts whence the smoke arose
> I met one walking.

One can hardly imagine a more vivid rendering of this experience: the German planes disappearing over the horizon, the dead leaves rattling over the asphalt. Souls wander the broken, burning city, looking for lost ones, lost homes, their own lost lives. The passage, a lengthy one, continues in the manner of Dante's *Inferno,* in occasionally rhyming triplets—an English approximation of Dante's terza rima. The poet encounters someone very like Dante himself, one of the several dead masters who presides over this poem. And it was Dante's work, as Eliot often suggested, to purify the dialect of the tribe.

The difficulty of doing this work of purification—finding the right words among so many that obscure realities instead of clarifying or embodying them—becomes a central theme in the final section of each quartet. In these memorable passages, Eliot speaks most nakedly, often personally, about the task of the artist. He writes about the struggle to express himself, and puts forward his understanding of what it would mean to write in a satisfactory way, as in "Burnt Norton," where he says:

> Words strain,
> Crack and sometimes break, under the burden,
> Under the tension, slip, slide, perish,
> Decay with imprecision, will not stay in place,
> Will not stay still.

Mortal words cannot, of course, compare with logos, the "Word in the desert," which was in the beginning, a word (and world) without end. "Burnt Norton" moves toward a kind of irresolute resolution, a brief standing on the hill, as when divine reality was glimpsed in the rose garden—a scene that Eliot recapitulates in the last section of this quartet with the figures of strange dream children who inhabit the garden and distract the speaker:

> Sudden in a shaft of sunlight
> Even while the dust moves
> There rises the hidden laughter
> Of children in the foliage
> Quick now, here, now, always—
> Ridiculous the waste sad time
> Stretching before and after.

This "waste sad time" is clock time, which extends backward from the "now" as well as forward from it, but which is ridiculous and empty—at least by comparison with now, which (to jump forward to "Little Gidding") "Is England and nowhere. Never and always."

In the final part of "East Coker," Eliot writes again with astonishing candor. I can think of no better description of the work of writing:

> So here I am, in the middle way, having had twenty years—
> Twenty years largely wasted, the years of *l'entre deux guerres*—
> Trying to learn to use words, and every attempt
> Is a wholly new start, and a different kind of failure
> Because one has only learnt to get the better of words
> For the thing one no longer has to say, or the way in which
> One is no longer disposed to say it. And so each venture
> Is a new beginning, a raid on the inarticulate

With shabby equipment always deteriorating
In the general mess of imprecision of feeling,
Undisciplined squads of emotion.

Dante reappears, covertly by allusion, in the first line just quoted, the poet in "the middle way," which recalls the opening of the *Inferno:* "Nel mezzo del camin di nostra vita / mi ritrovai per una selva oscura," In the middle of my road in my life's journey, I found myself in a dark wood.

Eliot's dark wood is verbal as well as spiritual. As a man of words, he has to search for those words, and the right arrangement of those words: the saving grace of language. But he understands the difficulty here. Language, at its best, points to silence, as he suggests in "Burnt Norton." But merely to say nothing is not to achieve silence. That is the paradox. One has to speak, to search out patterns, to scour the dark, in order to discover the chinks in time that reveal the light. This requires discipline and reading, which is part of that discipline.

Needless to say, allusions permeate *Four Quartets,* where one hears references to Saint John of the Cross, Dante, Dame Julian of Norwich, voices from Ecclesiastes and the Gospels, from the Bhagavad Gita and the Upanishads. Familiar compound ghosts appear and disappear, often obliquely. Eliot understood that language comes from language, and that the poet is always a guest at a great feast. He takes a helping and passes the serving dish. He fills his glass and passes the decanter. There are loaves and fishes in abundance, an endless supply of insight, a bounty of hints and guesses.

. . . . .

It is in the fifth section of "Little Gidding," the fourth quartet, that Eliot brings his exploration of writing to a point of near perfection, drawing on phrases and rhythms heard in the previous three poems:

> What we call the beginning is often the end
> And to make an end is to make a beginning.
> The end is where we start from. And every phrase
> And sentence that is right (where every word is at home,
> Taking its place to support the others,
> The word neither diffident nor ostentatious,
> An easy commerce of the old and the new,
> The common word exact without vulgarity,
> The formal word precise but not pedantic,
> The complete consort dancing together)
> Every phrase and every sentence is an end and a beginning,
> Every poem an epitaph.

It was this easy commerce of the old and new that distinguished Eliot's career from the beginning, and about which he theorized so brilliantly in "Tradition and the Individual Talent," the early essay that prefigures much of his later poetic practice. Eliot knew that one must learn from the past. One must read and listen, meditate, and allow for the old to refresh the new. And one must stand humbly before the past, as a beginner, always relearning old truths, always coming to the same moment of perception, again and again, before the passing of the cloud, the dimming of the vision, and the return to solitude and verbal confusion. The chatter of daily life distracts us from distraction but never satisfies or saves us. Only the right words in time can do that.

This brings me to the rather vast and dizzying questions I

posed at the outset. The answers to these questions will tell us why poetry matters, at least in part. So what is the human condition? How do we understand time and our place in the chronological cosmos? Do we have a purpose on this earth? What are the truths that literature and scripture can teach us? What role does poetry in particular have to play in helping us to understand these questions?

Eliot argues, convincingly for me, that life is not without purpose, neither empty of meaning nor without a discernable pattern. We need time and history to redeem the time and to transform hints and guesses into a clear vision. As he writes in "Little Gidding," "A people without history / Is not redeemed from time, for history is a pattern / Of timeless moments." Eliot directs us to respect silence in its perfected form, a condition which art anticipates in haphazardly beautiful ways. And so, in "Burnt Norton," he tells us:

> Only by the form, the pattern,
> Can words or music reach
> The stillness, as a Chinese jar still
> Moves perpetually in its stillness.

Eliot is never Panglossian, or overly optimistic, to say the least. The human condition as revealed in this sequence of poems is bleak indeed; there is war, poverty, illness, estrangement, and remorse. Eliot has put all of this before us. Yet I take comfort in Eliot's sources of comfort:

> After the kingfisher's wing
> Has answered light to light, and is silent, the light is still
> At the still point of the turning world.

The kingfisher is an allusion to Christ, and for Eliot, Christ is logos himself, the embodied Word in the desert. The world tree is the cross, the symbolic intersection of history with eternity: the timeless moment in time, the crux of reality. Eliot sees Christ as the culmination of spiritual questing. He sees the cross as a metaphor for the life of suffering that each must bear, and that he considers the appropriate burden for what we get in the end: a perfect silence in which everything comes clear. Eliot quotes stunningly—just one bold line, set off on its own, a stanza to itself, from the anonymous mystical text *The Cloud of Unknowing*:

> With the drawing of this Love and the voice of this Calling.

With this Love and this Calling both in capital letters, one can hardly miss the meaning: love is the restorative impulse, the antidote to war, to poverty, to hatred and remorse. This is love as charity (*caritas*). It is love in its worldliest incarnation as eros. It is love in all its divine and barely comprehensible beauty, glimpsed only sideways by those of us still in time, in the hints and guesses that pass before us.

"And the voice of this Calling"—this is the calling of the poet as well as the saint. It is the calling of each human being in the hard but rewarding search for meaning, the search for soul definition, which is also the search for community, as we gather, hand in hand, in the dance around the village fire that Eliot himself regards at sunset in the tiny village in Somerset where, centuries ago, his own journey began even before he came into fleshly existence. Eliot quotes here from a sixteenth-century book by his own distant ancestor and namesake, Sir Thomas Elyot:

                                          In that open field
If you do not come too close, if you do not come too close,
On a summer midnight, you can hear the music
Of the weak pipe and the little drum
And see them dancing around the bonfire
The association of man and woman
In daunsinge, signifying matrimonie—
A dignified and commodious sacrament.
Two and two, necessarye coniunctin,
Holding eche other by the hand or the arm
Whiche betokeneth concorde.

In all, *Four Quartets* draws together a lifetime of reading and contemplation by Eliot, and provides a unique synthesis of his thought. It is a densely allusive but in the end surprisingly straight-forward piece of writing. Although it is expressly Christian in outlook, there is a deeply ecumenical vision here, one that brings together insights from a variety of world religions and mytholo-gies. The sequence spins through the four seasons, the four ele-ments, taking hints and guesses from the four winds. It moves in history, in time, in the time of this poet and his residence on earth—stopping in Missouri, in Massachusetts, in the various English sites conjured here and there. But, most crucially, it offers us a pattern, a way out, which is the way up and the way down as well. It offers us, as the epigraph from Heraclitus promises, a communal sense of truth—a logos—that is always before us, ours for the taking.

conclusion

We are all one; our inconsequential
minds are much alike, and
circumstances so influence us that
it is something of an accident
that you are the reader and I
the writer—the unsure, ardent
writer—of these verses.

JORGE LUIS BORGES

Poetry does many things, as I have tried to suggest. For a start, it provides a language adequate to the experience of the writer and, perhaps, the reader (who are not so far apart as one might think, as Borges suggests). Poets may not be the "unacknowledged legislators of the world," as Shelley grandly declared, but poets are most certainly "the legislators of the un-acknowledged world," as George Oppen wittily countered. They peer into hidden places and speak for those who have no voice. They wander into the cities and forests, with eyes and ears open, and report on these experiences with astonishing candor and subtleness. They "purify the dialect of the tribe," as Eliot (after Mallarmé) put it, and they do so by using words carefully. They know that every word was once a picture, as Emerson suggested. In their poems, they refresh the language by returning words to their concrete roots.

Poets are not philosophers or linguists, and so they do not en-gage in forms of analysis associated with those disciplines; but they often suggest that language is the key to philosophic under-standing, believing (with Emerson) that connections exist between words and things, and that these alignments have a spiritual dimension. Words are symbols, and—as such—have resonance beyond their literal meanings. They gesture in directions that cannot be pinned down, and strike chords in the unconscious mind. This all gets very murky: many people do not believe in a world of "spirit," a word that smacks of dogma to them. Some prefer not to make distinctions between "mind" and "nature" or between "body" and "soul." Platonic dualism seems out of date, even bogus, in the twenty-first century. Yet poets persist in allowing for a spiritual world, in making associations that one might call "religious" in their poems, linking back to a source of inspiration, to God or whatever (in the words of Paul Tillich) one describes as one's ultimate concern.[1] One could, I think, adequately consider the spiritual dimensions of poetry in psychological terms as well, regarding its project as an attempt to link the conscious mind to deeper, even unconscious, levels of experience.

I myself consider poetry a form of religious as well as political thought. A poem, for me, is an interrogation of the world of spirit in nature. Poets look for occult connections and locate embodiments in the natural world for feelings and thoughts that one could describe as "spiritual" without ascribing them to any specific theology. Emerson himself, a perpetual touchstone for me, began life as a fairly orthodox minister in the Christian church; he evolved, through time, to become the founder of what Harold Bloom has called "the American religion." Bloom finds the core of that religion in one of the most eloquent passages in Emerson's *Nature:* "Our age is retrospective. It builds the sepulchers of the fathers. It writes biographies, histories, and criticism. The foregoing generations beheld God and nature face to face; we, through their eyes. Why should we also not enjoy an original relation to the universe?"[2]

This insistence on an "original relation to the universe," a fresh experience of the natural world, unmediated by tradition—represented by the "sepulchers" of biography, history, and criticism—seems relevant to poetry in general. Language mediates between physical and mental experience, as John Locke once suggested. But poetic language does so more intensely, finding reality in the language itself, in its intensified forms. It brings us closer to "God and nature," in Emerson's terms. At its best, it provides what the critic Geoffrey Hartman once called the unmediated vision. It doesn't stand in the way between reader and the world; it embodies the world.

Even Eliot's reverence for tradition can be accommodated in these Emersonian terms. Eliot insisted on the living aspect of the tradition and how it was modified by the addition of "the new (the really new) work of art." Eliot shattered that tradition into fragments and rebuilt a vision (however bleak) in *The Waste Land.* He found a fresh and more hopeful synthesis of tradition in *Four Quartets,* where he assembled a worldview from (mostly) Christian sources, adding a measure of Hindu and Buddhist insight. Yet he understood that, for most readers, self-reliance—Emerson's ultimate recourse—is a kind of fundamental ground, however insufficient in strict theological terms:

> For most of us, there is only the unattended
> Moment, the moment in and out of time,
> The distraction fit, lost in a shaft of sunlight,

The wild thyme unseen, or the winter lightning
Or the waterfall, or music heard so deeply
That it is not heard at all, but you are the music
While the music lasts.

Poetry matters because it provides this music, which at its best is heard so deeply that it approximates silence. Poetry matters because it serves up the substance of our lives, and becomes more than a mere articulation of experience—although that articulation alone is part of its usefulness. Its adequacy to experience, in fact, is profound and lasting in the many different ways I have suggested in this book. Mainly, it allows us to see ourselves freshly and keenly. It makes the invisible world visible. It transforms our politics by enhancing our ability to make comparisons and draw distinctions. It reanimates nature for us, connecting spirit and matter. It draws us more deeply into conversation with the traditions that we feed off, modify, and extend. In the end, it brings us closer to God, however we define that term. It provides, in some cases, a reason for life itself. "How gladly with proper words the soldier dies," writes Stevens, "If he must, or lives on the bread of faithful speech."

notes

CHAPTER ONE: DEFENDING POETRY

1. Plato, *Dialogues,* trans. Benjamin Jowett (Oxford: Clarendon, 1871). This text, like many of the works quoted in this chapter, is conveniently anthologized by William Harmon in *Classic Writings on Poetry* (New York: Columbia University Press, 2003), 3–29.

2. Aristotle, *Poetics,* trans. S. H. Butcher (New York: Macmillan, 1932). See Harmon, *Classic Writings,* 33–62.

3. *Horace on the Art of Poetry,* trans. C. Smart and E. H. Blakeney (London: Scholartis, 1928).

4. Gordon Williams, *Tradition and Originality in Roman Poetry* (Oxford: Clarendon, 1968), 357.

5. Horace, *Odes,* III, 1, translation mine.

6. *Longinus on the Sublime,* trans. W. Rhys Robert (London: Cambridge University Press, 1899). See Harmon, *Classic Writings,* 80–106.

7. T. S. Eliot, *Selected Essays* (New York: Harcourt, Brace and World, 1950), 200.

8. Sir Philip Sidney, *An Apologie for Poetrie,* ed. Edward Arber (London, 1858). See Harmon, *Classic Writings,* "The Defence of Poesy," 117–152.

9. William Wordsworth, "Observations Prefixed to *Lyrical Ballads*" (1800), in Harmon, *Classic Writings,* 279–296.

10. See M. H. Abrams, *The Mirror and the Lamp: Romantic Theory and the Critical Tradition* (New York: Oxford University Press, 1953). Abrams offers a thorough discussion of the influence of German critics on Romantic theory in England. Samuel Taylor Coleridge, *Biographia Literaria,* ed. George Watson (London: Dent, 1965), 173 and *passim.* See in particular chapter 14.

11. Abrams, *Mirror and the Lamp,* 222.

12. Thomas Love Peacock, "Four Ages of Poetry" (1820), and Percy Bysshe Shelley, "A Defence of Poety," in *Shelley's Defense of Poetry, and Browning's Essay on Shelley,* ed. H. F. B. Brett-Smith (Oxford: Blackwell, 1923). See Harmon, *Classic Writings,* 318–330, 351–374.

13. Ralph Waldo Emerson, "The Poet," in *Selections from Ralph Waldo Emerson,* ed. Stephen E. Whicher (Boston: Houghton Mifflin, 1957), 231.

14. Walt Whitman, *Leaves of Grass* (New York: Heritage, 1937), xxxix (preface to the 1855 edition).

15. "Emily Dickinson's Letters," ed. Thomas Wentworth Higginson, *Atlantic Monthly* (October 1891), 9. Numbers of Dickinson's poems refer to *The Complete Poems of Emily Dickinson,* ed. Thomas H. Johnson (Boston: Little, Brown, 1960).

16. Eliot, *Selected Essays,* 247.

17. T. S. Eliot, "Little Gidding," in *Four Quartets* (London: Faber, 1944); Robert Frost, *Collected Poems, Prose, and Plays* (New York: Library of America, 1995), 777.

18. Wallace Stevens, *The Necessary Angel: Essays on Reality and the Imagination* (London: Faber, 1951), 3–36.

19. Adrienne Rich, *On Lies, Secrets, and Silence: Selected Prose, 1966–1978* (New York: Norton, 1979), 34, 43.

20. Barbara Charlesworth Gelpi and Albert Gelpi, eds., *Adrienne Rich's Poetry* (New York: Norton, 1975), 119.

1. Ilham Dilman, "Fiction and Reality in the Arts," in Peter Lewis, *Wittgenstein, Aesthetics, and Philosophy* (London: Ashgate, 2004), 187.

2. One can see the influence of these philosophers in more recent thinkers, such as Hilary Putnam, John Searle, Saul Kripke, and others.

3. For a frank analysis of the difficulties linguists have encountered over the years in understanding how language functions see Noam Chomsky, *New Horizons in the Study of Language and Mind* (Cambridge: Cambridge University Press, 2000). In particular, see Chomsky's discussion of the so-called Minimalist Program, pp. 9–19.

4. Chomsky, *New Horizons,* 5.

5. Noam Chomsky, "Deep Structure, Surface Structure, and Semantic Interpretation," in *Semantics,* ed. Danny D. Steinberg and Leon J. Jakobovits (Cambridge: Cambridge University Press, 1968), 183–216.

6. Noam Chomsky, interview with Domenico Pacitti, in *Times Higher Educational Supplement* (March 24, 2000).

7. *The Great Dialogues of Plato,* trans. W. H. D. Rouse (New York: Mentor, 1956), 1041, 1090.

8. Lucretius, *De rerum natura,* quoted in M. H. Abrams, *The Mirror and the Lamp: Romantic Theory and the Critical Tradition* (New York: Oxford University Press, 1953), 79.

9. Abrams, *Mirror and the Lamp,* 78; John Dennis, quoted in Abrams, *Mirror and the Lamp,* 79.

10. John Stuart Mill, quoted in Abrams, *Mirror and the Lamp,* 136.

11. Ralph Waldo Emerson, "Nature," in *Selections from Ralph Waldo Emerson,* ed. Stephen E. Whicher (Boston: Houghton Mifflin, 1957), 31.

12. Louise Glück, *Proofs & Theories: Essays on Poetry* (New York: Ecco, 1994), 3–4.

13. George Orwell, "Politics and the English Language," in *Inside the Whale and Other Essays* (London: Penguin, 1957), 143–158.

CHAPTER THREE:
THE PERSONAL VOICE

1. Jack Heffron, *The Writer's Idea Book* (Cincinnati: Writer's Digest Books, 2000), 249.

2. Peter Elbow, *Writing with Power,* 2d ed. (New York: Oxford University Press, 1998); George Orwell, "Politics and the English Language," in *Inside the Whale and Other Essays* (London: Penguin, 1957), 143–158.

3. Robert Frost, *Collected Poems, Prose, and Plays* (New York: Library of America, 1995), 664.

4. Voice in this sense is related to the enterprise of "writing back" and what is called "domain mapping" in postcolonial theory, pioneered by Judith Butler and Homi Bhabha. See Judith Butler, *The Discursive Limits of Sex* (New York: Routledge, 1993) and *The Psychic Life of Power* (Stanford: Stanford University Press, 1996); Homi Bhabha, *The Location of Culture* (New York: Routledge, 1994). A good exposition of this area of discourse will be found in Patrick Colm Hogan, *Empire and Poetic Voice: Cognitive and Cultural Studies of Literary Tradition and Colonialism* (Albany: State University of New York Press, 2004).

5. W. B. Yeats, quoted in Norman Jeffares, *W. B. Yeats: Man and Poet* (London: Routledge and Kegan Paul, 1949), 163.

6. See Jay Parini, *Robert Frost: A Life* (New York: Henry Holt, 2000), for a detailed exploration of Frost's use of masks.

CHAPTER FOUR: THE
WAY OF METAPHOR

1. Robert Frost, "Education by Poetry," in Frost, *Collected Poems, Prose, and Plays* (New York: Library of America, 1995), 777.

2. Wallace Stevens, *The Necessary Angel: Essays on Reality and the Imagination* (London: Faber, 1951), 130.

3. See Umberto Eco, *The Open Work,* trans. Anna Cancogni (Cam-

bridge: Harvard University Press, 1989); Nelson Goodman, *Languages of Art* (Indianapolis: Hackett, 1976); George Lakoff and Mark Johnson, *Metaphors We Live By* (Chicago: University of Chicago Press, 1980); Miriam Taverniers, *Metaphor and Metaphorology: A Selective Genealogy of Philosophical and Linguistic Conceptions of Metaphor from Aristotle to the 1990s* (Ghent: Academia, 2002).

4. Aristotle, *Poetics,* trans. S. H. Butcher (New York: Macmillan, 1932), reprinted in William Harmon, *Classic Writings on Poetry* (New York: Columbia University Press, 2003), 33–62.

5. See I. A. Richards, *The Philosophy of Rhetoric* (New York: Oxford University Press, 1936).

6. See, for example, Jacques Derrida, "White Mythology: Metaphor in the Text of Philosophy," in *Margins of Philosophy,* trans. Alan Bass (Chicago: University of Chicago Press, 1982).

7. William Butler Yeats, *Selected Poems and Two Plays,* ed. M. L. Rosenthal (New York: Collier, 1962), 210.

8. See Elizabeth Langland, "Blake's Feminist Revision of Literary Tradition in 'The Sick Rose,'" in *Critical Paths: Blake and the Argument of Method,* ed. Dan Miller, Mark Bracher, and Donald Ault (Durham: Duke University Press, 1987), 225–243. For extended readings of "The Sick Rose" in the context of other poems by Blake, see also Northrop Frye, *Fearful Symmetry: A Study of William Blake* (Princeton: Princeton University Press, 1947), and Hazard Adams, *William Blake* (Seattle: University of Washington Press, 1963).

CHAPTER FIVE: TRADITION
AND ORIGINALITY

1. T. S. Eliot, "Tradition and the Individual Talent," in *The Sacred Wood: Essays on Poetry and Criticism* (London: Methuen, 1950), 50.

2. Gordon Williams, *Tradition and Originality in Roman Poetry* (Oxford: Clarendon, 1968), 250.

3. Johann Peter Eckermann, *Conversations of Goethe,* trans. John Oxenford, ed. J. K. Morehead (New York: Da Capo, 1998).

4. Harold Bloom, *The Anxiety of Influence* (New York: Oxford University Press, 1973), 70.

CHAPTER SIX: FORM AND FREEDOM

1. Gabriel Josipovici, *The World and the Book: A Study of Modern Fiction* (London: Macmillan, 1971), 309.

CHAPTER SEVEN: THE
POLITICS OF POETRY

1. Jerome Loving, *Walt Whitman: The Song of Himself* (Berkeley: University of California Press, 2000), 174.

2. "Emily Dickinson's Letters," ed. Thomas Wentworth Higginson, *Atlantic Monthly* (October 1891), 4.

3. Edmund Spenser, "A View of the Present State of Ireland," in *Spenser's Prose Works,* ed. Rudolf Gottfried (Baltimore: Johns Hopkins University Press, 1949), 124.

CHAPTER EIGHT: A NATURAL WORLD

1. William Empson, *English Pastoral Poetry* (New York: Norton, 1938), 10–11.

2. Wendell Berry, "Discipline and Hope," in *A Continuous Harmony: Essays Cultural and Agricultural* (New York: Harcourt, Brace, Jovanovich, 1972), 160.

3. Berry, "A Secular Pilgrimage," in *Continuous Harmony,* 15.

4. Alfred North Whitehead, *Science and the Modern World* (New York: Macmillan, 1925), 55, 156.

5. Ralph Waldo Emerson, "History," in Emerson, *Essays: First Series* (Boston: Houghton Mifflin, 1883), 34–35.

6. Gerard Manley Hopkins, *Poems and Prose,* ed. W. H. Gardner (Harmondsworth: Penguin, 1973), 123.

7. John Elder, *Imagining the Earth: Poetry and the Vision of Nature* (Hanover, N.H.: University Press of New England, 1985), 163, 40.

8. John F. Lynen, *The Pastoral Art of Robert Frost* (New Haven: Yale University Press, 1960), 189.

9. Gary Snyder, *Myths and Texts* (New York: New Directions, 1978), 23; Bernard W. Quetchenbach, *Back from the Far Field: American Nature Poetry in the Late Twentieth Century* (Charlottesville: University Press of Virginia, 2000), 160.

10. Janet McNew, "Mary Oliver and the Tradition of Romantic Nature Poetry," *Contemporary Literature* 30:1 (Spring 1989): 60, 75.

CONCLUSION

1. See Paul Tillich, *Dynamics of Faith* (New York: Harper and Row, 1957).

2. Ralph Waldo Emerson, "Nature," in *Selections from Ralph Waldo Emerson,* ed. Stephen E. Whicher (Boston: Houghton Mifflin, 1957), 31.

acknowledgments

I am grateful to many friends for reading this manuscript and offering comments. But special thanks must go to my editor, John Donatich, to my agent, Geri Thoma, and to Sam Pickering, Christopher Benfy, and John Elder—good friends and good readers. The detailed comments received from all of the above were helpful and generous. I'm also grateful to Julia Alvarez, Michael Collier, Paul Christensen, Alastair Reid, and others, for their encouragement and conversations. Devon Jersild, my wife, offered many useful suggestions, and I thank her as well.

index

comparison. *See* metaphor; simile; symbol

thinking and, xiii, 65, 66, 70, 74; pastoral mode and, 90, 136, 146–148; political conservatism of, 117, 118–121; on sound of poem, 43, 46; on tone, 55; tradition and, 147–148; voice and, 44, 54–56, 62; word's root meaning and, 37–38; on work of poet, 19. Works of: "Death of a Hired Man," 54; "Design," 37–38; "Directive," 147–148; "Education by Poetry," 66, 70; "For Once, Then, Something," 90, 146–148; "The Hill Wife," 54–55; "Home Burial," 54; "A Hundred Collars," 54; *A Masque of Mercy,* 55; *New Hampshire,* 55; "New Hampshire," 118; *North of Boston,* 54; "Provide, Provide," 118–119; "Revelation," 148; "The Road Not Taken," 55; "Snow," 55; "Two Tramps in Mud Time," 119–121

Frye, Northrop, 72

Galileo, 30
German Romanticism, 12, 36
Ginsberg, Allen, 4, 6, 131; *Howl,* 4
Glück, Louise, xii, 65, 133, 136, 149, 153; "Education of Poet," 50; "Flowering Plum," xv; "Messenger," 74
gnosticism, 152
Goethe, Johann Wolfgang von, 85–87
Gonne, Maud, 51, 118
Goodman, Nelson, 68

Graham, Jorie, 43, 149; "Self-Portrait as the Gesture Between Them," 140
grammar, 25, 28–29
Great Depression, 118
Great War, 18, 20, 118, 131
Greek thought. *See* classical world
grief, expression of, 102
group-defining voice, 47–48

harmony, 4–5
Harris, Zellig, 28
Hass, Robert, 149
Havens, R. D., *The Influence of Milton on English Poetry,* 88
Haydn, Franz Joseph, 158
Heaney, Seamus, 48, 89–90, 115; "Personal Helicon," 90
Heffron, Jack, *The Writer's Idea Book,* 45
Heidegger, Martin, 25–26
hell imagery, 160
Heraclitus, 157, 158, 163, 175
Herbert, George, 141
Herder, J. G., 12
Hermetic Students of the Golden Dawn, 51
heroism, 131
Higginson, Thomas Wentworth, 123–124
Hinduism, xv, 156, 158, 162, 165, 171
history, 173, 174
Holinshed, Raphael, *Chronicles,* 83
Homer, 2–3, 7, 8, 48, 103–104; *Iliad,* 3, 84, 103; *Odyssey,* 103

Hopkins, Gerard Manley: as literary influence, 90; nature poetry and, 141–142; on poetic language, 35–36, 58, 152; sprung rhythm and, 105. Works of: "Pied Beauty," 141–142; "Spring," 142

Horace, 4, 5, 8, 32, 85; *Ars poetica,* 5–6

Howe, Susan, 49

Hughes, Langston, 121, 124–126; "Dinner Guest: Me," 124–125; "Harlem," 128; "Un-American Investigations," 125; "Warning," 125

Hughes, Ted, 48

Humankind: analogical thinking and, 69; calling of, 174; language capacity of, 24, 31–32; nature and, 41–42, 135–136, 138–139, 145–146, 148. *See also* life; spirit

human rights, 127

"hybridity" (culture mixing), 47

hymns, 102

iambic pentameter, 106, 107

ideal, 2, 9, 10, 22, 32; Greek emulation of, 84–85; nature as imitation of, 2, 9, 10, 32

ideas, verbalization of, 24, 31–32

identity, 10, 47. *See also* voice

identity politics, 47, 117

images: Eliot's use of, 18, 160, 161–163, 166–167; embodying state of mind, 39–40; from nature, 140–141, 148; in poetic language, 35–36, 39; real vs. mental, xii–xiii. *See also* metaphor; symbol

imagination: analogy between nature and, 42, 65, 133; Coleridge's two-part conception of, 13–14, 59; poetry's enlargement of, 15; relationship between reality and, 20–21, 22, 67, 76, 77

Imagists, 110–111

imitation (mimesis): language theory and, 32–33; Plato on, 2, 9, 10, 32; poetic vision vs., 11; poetry seen as, 2, 4, 5–6, 9, 10; of poet's precursors, 84–85, 98

indirection, 123

"individual talent" (Eliot term), xiv, 80

individual voice. *See* voice

infinity, 42; discrete, 30–31

influences. *See* tradition

"inscape" (Hopkins term), 152

inspiration, xv, xvi, 142, 156

internal rhyme, 108, 109

interpretation, 73–74

Iraq War, 121

Ireland, 50, 51, 53, 117–118, 130

irony, 123

Italian language, 107, 108

James, Henry, 60

James, William, 27

Jeffers, Robinson, 136

John, Gospel of, 157, 158

John of the Cross, Saint, 171

Johnson, Mark, 68, 69

personality and, 52, 62; poetic vs. public, 44, 45–46, 53, 58, 62–63

Voigt, Ellen Bryant, 149

Voltaire, 127

vowels, 104–105, 108, 110

Wagner, Richard, 61

war, 7, 18; poets' responses to, 3, 4, 19–20, 21, 118, 126, 130, 131, 168–169, 174; political metaphors and, xiii

Warren, Robert Penn, "Blow, West Wind," 95–96, 97, 98

Waste Land (Eliot), 18, 35, 82–83; Frost's answer to, 147–148; as lyric compilation, 35; mosaic of quotations in, 83; as multivoiced, 50, 60–61

"Western wind, when wilt thou blow" (anon.), 94, 95, 97–98

wheel of life, 158, 162, 165, 167

Whitehead, Alfred North, *Science and the Modern World,* 138–139

White House, "Poetry and the American Voice" (proposed 2003 symposium), 121

Whitman, Walt, xii, 138; autobiographical epic and, 35; free verse and, 108, 109–110; natural world and, 16–17, 141, 142–145, 150; poetic political expression and, 121–123; voice and, 58, 117. Works of: "Calamus," 121; "From Montauk Point," 143–144; *Leaves of Grass,* 16–17, 122, 143–145; "A Noiseless Patient Spider,"

109–110; "Roots and leaves themselves alone," 143; "A Song of Joys," 143; *Song of Myself,* 16, 35, 58, 109, 122, 144–145; "Song of the Open Road," 143; "A Song of the Rolling Earth," 143

Williams, Gordon, 6; *Tradition and Originality in Roman Poetry,* 85

Williams, William Carlos, 111–113; "To a Poor Old Woman," 112–113

wisdom literature, 157

Wittgenstein, Ludwig, xii, 25–26; *Philosophical Investigations,* 26

women's status, 123–124

Woolf, Virginia, xvi

Word. *See* logos

words, 25; in context, 40–41; denotation and connotation of, 40; ideas expressed through, 24; as metaphors, 37, 69–70; as palimpsests, 80, 96; pictorial origins of, 16, 37; poet's choice of, 172; as poet's raw material, 40; as representing things, 26, 32–33, 39; rhyme and, 107–108; root meaning of, xii, 37–38

Wordsworth, William, 108; autobiographical epic and, 35, 48; literary influences and, 88, 91–94; on meaning/purpose of poetry, 11–12, 13, 14; pastoral mode and, 136, 141, 152; voice and, 56–57, 58. Works of: "London, 1802," 91–94; preface to *Lyrical Ballads,* 11–12; *The Prelude,* 35, 48, 56–57, 58, 152

credits

I thank the copyright holders for permission to reprint the following poems or poem extracts.

Elizabeth Bishop, excerpts from "The Riverman" and "Seascape," from *The Complete Poems, 1926–1979*. Copyright © 1965 by Elizabeth Bishop, copyright © 1979, 1983 by Alice Helen Methfessel. Reprinted with the permission of Farrar, Straus & Giroux, LLC.

Emily Dickinson, "A word is dead," "Much Madness is divinest Sense—," and excerpts from "This was a Poet—It is That" and "The Poets light but Lamps," from *The Poems of Emily Dickinson*, edited by Thomas H. Johnson. Copyright 1945, 1951, © 1955, 1979, 1983 by the President and Fellows of Harvard College. Reprinted with the permission of the Belknap Press of Harvard University Press and the Trustees of Amherst College.

Richard Eberhart, "For a Lamb," from *Collected Poems 1930–1986*. Copyright © 1988 by Richard Eberhart. Reprinted with the permission of Oxford University Press, Ltd.

T. S. Eliot, excerpts from "East Coker," "Burnt Norton," "The Dry Salvages," and "Little Gidding," from *Four Quartets*, from *T. S. Eliot: The Complete Poems and Plays, 1909–1950*. Copyright 1922, 1925, 1927, 1941 by T. S. Eliot. Reprinted with the permission of Harcourt, Inc., and Faber and Faber, Ltd.

Robert Frost, excerpts from "Design," "The Road Less Taken," "Provide, Provide," "Two Tramps in Mudtime," and "Directive," from *The Poetry of Robert Frost*, edited by Edward Connery Lathem. Copyright 1936, 1942 by Robert Frost, copyright 1947, © 1969 by Henry Holt and Company, copyright © 1964, 1975 by Lesley Frost Ballantine. Reprinted by permission of Henry Holt and Company, LLC, and Random House (UK) Ltd.

Louise Glück, excerpts from "Gemini" and "Mock Orange," from *The First Four Books of Poems.* Copyright © 1995 by Louise Glück. Reprinted with the permission of HarperCollins Publishers and Carcanet Press, Ltd.

Jorie Graham, excerpt from "Manifest Destiny," from *Materialism.* Copyright © 1993 by Jorie Graham. Reprinted with the permission of HarperCollins Publishers.

Langston Hughes, excerpts from "Dinner Guest: Me," "Un-American Investigators," "Ku Klux," and "Warning," from *Collected Poems.* Copyright 1936 and renewed copyright © 1964 by Langston Hughes, copyright © 1994 by the Estate of Langston Hughes. Reprinted with the permission of Alfred A. Knopf, a division of Random House, Inc., and Harold Ober Associates.

Les Murray, excerpt from "Poetry and Religion," from *The Daylight Moon.* Copyright © 1988 by Les Murray. Reprinted with the permission of Persea Books, Inc., Carcanet Press, Ltd., and Margaret Connolly & Associates P/L.

Mary Oliver, "Poppies," from *New and Selected Poems.* Copyright © 1992 by Mary Oliver. Reprinted with the permission of Beacon Press, Boston.

Jay Parini, "I Was There," from *House of Days.* Copyright © 1997 by Jay Parini. Reprinted with the permission of Henry Holt and Company, LLC.

Adrienne Rich, excerpt from "North American Time" (Part III), from *Your Native Land, Your Life.* Copyright © 2002, 1986 by Adrienne Rich. Reprinted with the permission of the author and W. W. Norton & Company, Inc.

Wallace Stevens, "The Motive for Metaphor" and excerpt from "The Idea of Order at Key West," from *The Collected Poems of Wallace Stevens.* Copyright 1923, 1936, 1942, 1947, 1954 by Wallace Stevens, renewed 1951 by Wallace Stevens, copyright © 1964, 1970, 1975, 1982 by Holly Stevens. Reprinted with the permission of Alfred A. Knopf, a division of Random House, Inc.

Robert Penn Warren, "Blow, West Wind," from *The Collected Poems* (Baton Rouge: Louisiana State University Press, 1998). Reprinted with the permission of the William Morris Agency, LLC, on behalf of the Estate of the Author.

William Carlos Williams, "To a Poor Old Woman," from *The Collected Poems of William Carlos Williams, Volume 1, 1909–1939,* edited by Christopher MacGowan. Copyright 1938, 1944, 1945 by William Carlos Williams. Reprinted with the permission of New Directions Publishing Corporation and Carcanet Press, Ltd.

William Butler Yeats, "The Mask," from *The Poems of W. B. Yeats: A New Edition,* edited by Richard J. Finneran. Reprinted with the permission of A. P. Watt, Ltd., on behalf of Gráinne Yeats, Executrix of the Estate of Michael Butler Yeats.

Jay Parini, a poet and novelist, is Axinn Professor of English at Middlebury College. His fifth book of poems was *The Art of Subtraction: New and Selected Poems* (2005). He has published six novels, including *The Last Station* (1990) and *Benjamin's Crossing* (1997), a critical study of Theodore Roethke, and a volume of essays on literature and politics, as well as biographies of John Steinbeck, Robert Frost, and William Faulkner. *The Art of Teaching* appeared in 2005. He writes regularly for various publications, including the *Chronicle of Higher Education* and *The Guardian.*